Designing for the Dancer

DESIGNING FOR THE DANCER

ROY STRONG
IVOR GUEST
RICHARD BUCKLE
BARRY KAY
LIZ DA COSTA

FOREWORD BY DAME ALICIA MARKOVA

universe

381 PARK AVENUE SOUTH · NEW YORK, N.Y. 10016

Book design by Fred Price
Design and production services by Elron Press Ltd., London.
Printed and bound in Great Britain by M & A Thomson Litho Ltd., East Kilbride.
Typeset in Palatino by Inforum Ltd., Portsmouth.

Strong, Roy
    Designing for the dancer.
    1. Ballet – Costume – History
    I. Title   II. Buckle, Richard
    III. Guest, Ivor
    792.8'026   GT1741

    ISBN 0-904499-11-1

TITLE PAGE:
The early Sylphide silhouette. Marie Taglioni in *La Sylphide*, 1834
Department of Prints and Drawings, V & A

FRONT COVER: (*left to right*)
Attributed to the Francini. Design for dancer's costume c.1605–10
Costume designed by Jean-Baptiste Martin for 'paysanne galante' c.1750
Design by Bakst for Anna Pavlova in *Dance Hindoo*

BACK COVER: (*left ro right*)
Design for *Solo Ride*
The anacreontic ballet in Romantic guise. Marie Taglioni in *Flore
et Zéphire*. Lithograph by R.J. Lane from a drawing by A.E. Chalon, 1831
Isadora. Act II (1927). Costume design. Royal Ballet 1981

CONTENTS

Foreword

7

Dress as Hieroglyph: Costume in the Ballet de Cour

9

Costume and the Nineteenth Century Dancer

33

Modern Ballet Design: 1909–1980

95

On Designing for Ballet Today: Barry Kay

97

On Designing for Ballet Today: Liz da Costa

107

FOREWORD

Dame Alicia Markova DBE DMus

In the following pages you will discover a most interesting, informative and rewarding history of designing for the dancer.

Many years ago I had the great good fortune to be instructed and guided in the arts by a real artistic genius, Serge Diaghilev. I became aware of the importance of design and its influence, not only in the theatre, but in other mediums as well as in everyday living. I acquired my practical knowledge by being lucky enough to work with many great painters and designers during my career and had the good sense to listen and learn from them.

Designing for the dancer has always been a fascinating subject since dancers first began expressing their emotions through movement. Many different designers have contributed a variety of trends and styles, all influenced by the choreography and technique of their time. Through the centuries we have seen skirts rise from the instep of the female dancer to disappear completely. Likewise, the male dancer has also been relieved of his heavy and restricting clothes.

I often feel the greatest influence towards design came in the nineteenth century from two Frenchmen, Monsieur Maillot and Jules Leotard when they gave us tights and leotards which to this day have become the traditional clothes for dancers worldwide.

15 February 1981

Dress as Hieroglyph: Costume in the Ballet de Cour

ROY STRONG

The *ballet de cour* was essentially a creation of the renaissance. Man the microcosm, the being who could rise to the stars or sink to the level of the brute beasts, was the focal point of a universe divinely structured according to number and proportion. Both renaissance platonism and hermetism cast man as a wonder worker who could, by putting himself at tune with the magical universe, achieve greater control over both it and his own destiny. The rise and decline of the *ballet de cour* coincides exactly with this era of man the microcosm, a belief that had a tremendous hold, in spite of the discoveries of Copernicus, Galileo and Kepler, until the close of the seventeenth century. By using music that imitated exactly the proportions of the harmony of the spheres sixteenth century man believed that he could attract planetary influences. Dance in itself was an imitation of the movement of the heavens. To combine both would produce an art form of extraordinary power, for, as Mersenne wrote in his *L'Harmonie Universelle* (1626), 'L'Auteur de l'Univers qui est le grand maistre du Balet'. The *ballet de cour* was a profound expression of one of the intellectual quests of the age, the revival of antique drama in which music, poetry, painting and the dance were fused. Broadly speaking this was the philosophical urge behind the creation of many new festival forms throughout the Europe of the renaissance from opera to the allegorical tournament. In France the poets and philosophers of the academies of the late sixteenth century found theirs in what was to be the direct ancestor of our modern ballet.

The French *ballet de cour*

The *ballet de cour* was a creation of the Valois court, evolving out of the complex varieties of entertainment that made up what was known as a set of *magnificences*. The latter stretched over a series of days and included masquerades, fighting on foot at the barriers, a water fête, and a tourney, all of which were designed to mark a particular political event and, under the presiding genius of the Queen Mother, Catherine de' Medici, were aimed to unite the divided Protestant and Catholic nobility in loyalty to the Crown. The first set of these *magnificences* was staged at Chenonçeaux in 1563 and the last celebrated the marriage of the Duc de Joyeuse in 1581. During these two decades the dance element in them was gradually to increase, under the impact of the poets and musicians who gave expression to the ideas of the theorists of the Academy and who believed in the revival and re-

creation of 'ancient music' and 'ancient poetry'. This programme included attempts to re-stage 'ancient dancing', thus achieving the humanist aim of uniting all these art forms once again into the ancient mode. Such an objective coincided with the Queen Mother's predilection, born of her Italian origins, for choreographed dances and these always formed a prominent feature in any contribution by her to a series of *magnificences*. Two sets of visual evidence give us an unrivalled picture of the background to the birth of the *ballet de cour*: the famous series of tapestries now in the Uffizi, known as the Valois Tapestries, and the drawings closely connected with them by the artist, Antoine Caron, who actually designed costumes and decor for two sets of *magnificences*.

The *ballet de cour* may be said to have been born as part of a water fête, one of the *magnificences* that took place at Bayonne in 1565 on the border of France and Spain whither the court had travelled so that Catherine de' Medici might meet her daughter, Elizabeth, wife of Philip II of Spain. Embarking on a boat constructed to look like a castle the royal party sailed through a series of canals to an island on which a banqueting house had been erected. *En route* fearsome monsters, symbolising the evils of war, were vanquished and on arrival the party was welcomed by the bucolic sight of shepherds and shepherdesses in the costumes of the provinces of France engaged in peaceful country dancing. And this we can see in both the tapestry and drawing depicting the event. A banquet followed, after which violinists struck up the music for nine nymphs, divided into a leader and two sets of four dancers wearing identical costumes, who entered from a rock and danced a ballet. This fête was Catherine's own contribution and there is vivid pictorial evidence for everything except the ballet.

We have no picture either of the ballet staged seven years later in 1572 on the occasion of the festivals for the marriage of Marguerite de Valois to Henry of Navarre. This time it was the finale to a barriers entitled *Le Paradis d'Amour*, in which the king and his brothers defended and eventually led out twelve nymphs from the Elysian Fields and joined them in dancing a complicated ballet that lasted more than an hour. These *magnificences* were rudely interrupted by the Massacre of St. Bartholemew and, although we have no pictures of the performers in *Le Paradis d'Amour*, the men would have been in knightly combat dress, certainly shedding their armour, but retaining the plumed helmet and embroidered bases or skirt. Male costume in the *ballet de cour* was emphatically related to tournament fancy dress. Out of this emerged the familiar silhouette which was to last until the end of the *ancien régime*.

A year later Paris was once more *en fête*, this time to receive ambassadors from Poland who had elected one of Catherine's sons, the future Henry III, as King. The climax to these festivals was the first full length ballet as such, the *Ballet of the Provinces of France*. This was staged by the Queen Mother in a temporary hall erected in the gardens of the Tuileries Palace. Sixteen ladies of the court, attired as the provinces, entered on a silver rock. Having toured the hall, they descended to dance a ballet that lasted more than an hour to music played by Apollo and the Muses. Nothing quite like it in the way of sustained choreography had ever been seen before and the Poles exclaimed that 'le bal de France estoit chose impossible à contrefaire à tous les rois de la terre'. The Valois Tapestry depicts the court ball that followed but a feeble woodcut in the official account of the entertainment pro-

The Ballet of the Provinces of France, 1573. Sixteen court ladies led by Marguerite de Valois, dance in a ballet. Woodcut. Jean Dorat: *Magnificentissimi Spectaculi. British Library*

vides us with the earliest picture that we have of dancers arranged in a figure and, at the same time, with the earliest evidence of French ballet costume. The ladies are dressed in two sets of eight identical costumes, which are court dresses of the period minus the train which the ladies in the court ball that followed are wearing. As in the case of men's ballet costume this establishes features that were to last down to 1789. Firstly the relationship of ballet costume to contemporary fashion, secondly the necessity for shorter skirts to facilitate movement and lastly the rule that the dancers were dressed *en suite*, something that was essential to visually emphasise the geometric patterns made by the dancers as they were looked down on from the tiered arena theatre.

The climax of Valois festival art was the set of *magnificences* to mark the wedding of the Duc de Joyeuse to the sister of Henry III's queen, Louise de Lorraine. In the midst of political chaos and economic ruin, the Crown was to expend a million écus on the fêtes. Ironically Catherine's own entertainment was never performed but her life's work found expression in a landmark for the *ballet de cour*, the entertainment staged by her daughter-in-law, *Le Ballet Comique de la Reyne*. Not only do we have the text but illustrations of what this momentous production actually looked like. As in the case of the previous spectacles it was an arena theatre with scenery scattered around the hall and the spectators sat on tiered seats on three sides. The plot of the Ballet was far more complex than 1573, telling the story of the defeat of the enchantress Circe, symbol of the evils of the passions, by the forces of Reason and the Rational Soul, represented in the final battle by the Cardinal Virtues and Minerva. The plot was developed through a series of *entrées*. One was of Queen Louise and her ladies, who entered on a chariot like a fountain and who descended to dance a ballet of thirteen figures until rendered spellbound by Circe. At the close of the ballet Minerva, Goddess of Reason and Wisdom, vanquished the enchantress and Queen Louise and her ladies were released to dance a ballet of forty geometric figures, expressing the mutation of the elements and seasons. The top half of the costumes of these ladies can be seen in the engraving and once again they are attired alike in a fanciful variant of contemporary dress.

In one aspect the Ballet Comique was an allegory of the religious wars which, subsequent to 1581, totally engulfed France and destroyed Valois court civilisation. We now have to move on over twenty years into the new century and its revival at the court of Henry IV. That the development of the *ballet de cour* should coincide with the revival of the monarchy was natural for the two were inextricably intertwined. The choreographic origins of the *ballet de cour* were Italian and the two most famous Valois ballets were the work of Balthasar de Beaujoyeulx, an Italian dancing master and choreographer. He prob-

ably choreographed *Le Paradis d'Amour* and certainly the ballets of 1573 and 1581. But ballet could never have emerged as *the* festival form ideally expressive of the new age of absolutism without being also a profound expression of renaissance ideas on order and harmony. For renaissance man dance reflected the structure of a universe based on number; it mirrored the progression of the seasons, the mutation of the elements and the circling of

Le Balet Comique de la Reyne, 1581. Entry of the Fountain Chariot bearing Queen Louise of Lorraine and her ladies as the dancers. Woodcut. *National Art Library, V & A (above left)*

Le Balet Comique de la Reyne, 1581. Entry of the Dryads. Woodcut. *National Art Library, V & A (above right)*

Le Balet Comique de la Reyne, 1581. Entry of the Tritons. *National Art Library, V & A (below left)*

Le Balet Comique de la Reyne, 1581. Entry of the Four Cardinal Virtues. *National Art Library, V & A (below right)*

the heavens. In other words the ballet emerged as the epitome in microcosm of the harmony of a correctly ordered body politic. By the middle of the seventeenth century, when Louis XIV appeared as *le Roi Soleil* it was more than a convenient pseudonym, it embodied the adoption of the post-Copernican system to the structure of the French state.

With the re-establishment of the French monarchy after the religious wars, the ballet was systematically developed first by Richelieu, then Mazarin and finally Louis XIV as a means whereby to exalt the power and order of the crown as the symbol of the nation's greatness. Although increasingly elaborate the structure was always the same, a series of half-danced, half-mimed *entrées* in the main of comic characters, often representing the opposition, followed by a triumph expressed in a prolonged ballet by royal and noble dancers, the whole embraced within an overall plot, based on legendary, chivalrous or classical mythology, which related allegorically to political events of the time. The most significant

visual development was the abandonment of the arena stage in favour of the proscenium arch and the introduction of scenery based on renaissance optical principles as evolved in the Florentine *intermezzi*. Single viewpoint perspective also magnified the monarch who occupied the focal point of the lines of vision either as participant or as viewer from the throne. This development began with the arrival of the Florentine engineers, Francesco and Tommaso Francini, who from *c.* 1610 onwards introduced the proscenium, a front curtain and also experimented with *periaktoi* and other machinery to effect changes of scene.

The visual evidence for the *ballet de cour* down to *c.* 1625 is frugal and uneven. There are, for example, designs for costumes which are difficult to date. A series of twenty such are preserved in the Victoria & Albert Museum in a volume which came from the *Garde Meuble* and which bears the French royal arms of *c.* 1635–70. They seem certainly to be by an Italian artist working in France and derive directly from the tradition of theatrical costume design established by Buontalenti for Medici court festivals. They are very early seventeenth century in date and logically ought to be by the Francini. Further research may establish this to be the fact. We only know of their work much later in the important series of engravings

Dancer, c. 1605–10. Attributed to the Francini. *Department of Prints & Drawings, V & A (left)*

Satyr, c. 1605–10. Attributed to the Francini. *Department of Prints & Drawings, V & A*

Le Ballet de la Délivrance de Renaud, 1617. Première Entrée.
Bibliothèque Nationale (above)

Le Ballet de la Délivrance de Renaud, 1617. The Monsters
Metamorphosed. *Bibliothèque Nationale (above right)*

Le Ballet de la Délivrance de Renaud, 1617. The grand Ballet of
Fourteen dancers led by Louis XIII. Woodcut. *Bibliothèque
Nationale*

depicting *Le Ballet de la délivrance de Renaud* danced in
January 1617. These are of immense importance offering
us the first dated material since 1581 on the development
of both ballet costume and decor. The ballet uses an
episode in Tasso as a vehicle to re-assert in the language
of festival the authority of the young Louis XIII against
the dominance of his mother and her advisers, the Con-
cini. The scenery was by the Francini and also presumably the costumes. In the former use was made of *periaktoi*. The ballet opened with a curtain falling to reveal a
mountain full of demons who held Renaud captive. Each
dress was expressive of the vice each demon represented.
The series of engravings depicting these introduces us to
a new element in characterisation and dress which was to
become a distinctive feature of the *ballet de cour* under the
Bourbons. The engraving of three of these demons plus
Renaud that made up the *première entrée*, for instance,
catches this strongly idiosyncratic feature of French *ballet
de cour* dress, the inventiveness of designers in incor-

porating the most bizarre attributes into costume in order to make the figure identifiable to the audience. This is essentially an expression of the mannerist imagination and the equivalent in terms of costume design to the painted fantasies of an Arcimboldo. In these costumes we see the silhouette of tournament dress preserved but incorporated, in the case of the Fire Demon, into a collage of flames. The Water Demon is encased in bullrushes and the Air Demon has wings and a bonnet atop a funnel on his head. The comic potentialities of this kind of costume were to be highly developed after 1620.

The scene then changed to an enchanted garden with the fountain of Armide where Renaud was made eventually to realise his voluptuous enslavement. The enchantress summoned up more demons, this time in the form of monsters whom she metamorphosed into ridiculous

old people in old-fashioned dress who danced a comic *entrée*. Finally Renaud escaped and returned to the path of virtue by means of a hermit and the ballet closed with a tableau, in opposition to that with which it opened, being one of virtue, revealing the crusader king Godefroy with his knights who descended to dance the grand ballet. Louis XIII as Godefroy led the fourteen dancers who, as was customary, were all masked and dressed alike in helmets with winged birds from which arose vase aigrettes, a doublet cut to resemble a cuirass and the bases of tournament dress decorated with swags, the whole designed to be *à l'antique* in mood. Emphasis in these grand ballet costumes was always on richness and variety, the fabrics being of satin, taffeta, silk and brocade covered with embroidery, precious stones and pearls. Lit by candles and torches the effect must have been one of glittering splendour.

From 1620 to 1636 the serious political *ballet de cour* fell into disfavour and was replaced by a series of burlesque ballets whose intent was to hold up, by means of an infinity of *entrées*, a distorting glass to society in which its modes, manners and morals were subject to ridicule.

Le Ballet de la Dovairière de Billebahaut, 1626. Entrée of the Great Cham. *Musée du Louvre*

Le Ballet de la Douairière de Billebahaut 1626. Entrée of the Hermaphrodites. *Musée du Louvre*

These developed the character dancing-acting to a high pitch and great use was made of professional dancers and acrobats with a consequent diminution of the role of the aristocratic amateur. The Louvre and the Bibliothèque Nationale contain a marvellous series of drawings of three of these ballets whose visual impact depended on the inventiveness and wit of the costume designer and in which scenery seems to have played a lesser part. That designer was a Frenchman, Daniel Rabel, whom Michel de Marolles rightly praised as excelling:

A former des dessins pour des jeux de balet,
Ses crayons achevez ne portoient rien de laid,
D'une maniere fine et d'un air agreable.

The three ballets for which we have a complete record are *Le Ballet des Fées des forêts de Saint-Germain* (1625), *Le Ballet de la Douairière de Billebahaut* (1626) and *Le Ballet du chasteau du Bicêtre* (1632). These establish Rabel as a great costume designer with an unfailing sense of wit and absurdity whose sources are as varied as medieval grotesques and drolleries, the *commedia dell'arte* and the costume manuals of Vecellio and others.

Le Ballet Royal du grand bal de la Douairière de Billebahaut was probably a satire on Marguerite de Valois in old age. In it a hideous old dowager gives a ball to which come the follies of the four corners of the world. America, for instance, was headed by King Atabalipa with a train of parrot catchers, by people who are half men and half women and by musicians disguised as bagpipers escorting an extraordinary upright xylophone on wheels. Africa was heralded by *le Grand Cacique* riding on an elephant followed by the Great Cham on a camel's back. In *Le Ballet du Chasteau de Bicêtre* the old castle has been demolished to make way for a hospital for cripples and the *entrées* consisted of shrouded ghosts from the grave or mysterious phantom knights. The drawings recording these satirical *entrées* remain one of the most evocative pictures of French court entertainment at its most light-hearted and frivolous. As a phase it proved to be transitory.

The political ballet was revived with force by Cardinal Richelieu between 1635 and his death in 1642. Ballet, along with other forms of theatre, became a means whereby to promote the cult of the monarchy and its plots drew on myth, legend and history to focus public attention on the triumph of the crown. The most important of these was *Le Ballet de la Prospérité des armes de la France* danced in 1641. Its innovations were to establish the

Le Ballet de la Douairière de Billebahaut 1626. Entrée of Le Grand Cacique. Watercolour. *Musée du Louvre*

Le Ballet de la Douairière de Billebahaut 1626. Entrée of the Dowager. Watercolour. Musée du Louvre

Le Ballet de la Douairière de Billebahaut 1626. Entrée of her lovers and servants. Watercolour. *Musée du Louvre*

Le Ballet de la Douairière de Billebahaut 1626. Entrée of the Great Turk. Watercolour. *Musée du Louvre*

norm for the remainder of *le grand siècle* and as such it is a landmark in the evolution of *ballet de cour*. It opened with Harmony suspended in a cloud singing of the peace and order of Louis XIII's France. This in itself was a reversal of the order of the old political ballets which began with disorder and moved by a series of encounters towards order and its achievement in the body politic. Pluto, Proserpina and the gods of the underworld appeared to disturb this peace and the first act was devoted to an allegorical exposition of the virtues of internal stability. The fact that the ballet was divided into acts was also new, as was the representation on stage of the recent victories by the French forces over the Spanish. The ballet reached its climax with the whole of Olympus singing the praises of the Gallic Hercules (Louis XIII) and closed, not with the dancers descending into an arena to perform a grand ballet, but with a vision of a glorious throne room for the King and Queen. A court ball followed but only subsequently. In other words, the break between the stage and audience was achieved because ideologically it no longer represented anything. The ballet did not express as formerly an aspiration to order which spread out from the stage by means of the arena and the linking

of performance and onlookers. The performance opened with it as *fait accompli*. From this decision followed a choreographic revolution signalling the end of the old figured dances, which were looked down upon from tiered seats around the room, and the development of choreography to be viewed from an auditorium on an elevated stage as we do today. This had enormous long term consequences as the century progressed, firstly the burlesque *entrées* were increasingly executed by professional dancers and acrobats, and secondly, the closing society dances having by this change been considerably truncated, the main dancing became increasingly concerned with interpretation of character and action, thus paving the way for the developments that were to take place under Noverre.

Louis XIII died in 1643 and two years later Cardinal Mazarin imported the great Italian scenographer, Giacomo Torelli. The opera *La Finta Pazza* staged that year created a sensation by introducing the baroque theatre of illusion, already pioneered by Richelieu, at its sophisticated apogée and confirmed the direction of the ballet towards a preoccupation with dazzling scenic spectacle dependent on sudden changes and transformations. The ballet continued to fulfil its political function, emphasised by the skill of the young Louis XIV as a dancer in a whole series of ballets from *Le Ballet des Fêtes de Bacchus* (1651) onwards. In 1651 Louis actually appeared for the first

Le Ballet des Fées des Forêts de Saint Germain 1625. Grand Ballet. *Bibliothèque Nationale*

time on stage in his most celebrated guise as *le Roi Soleil* in the *Ballet de la Nuit*. The last work Torelli was to design was the opera-ballet *Les Noces de Peleus et Thetis* (1654), after which he returned to Venice. Torelli was succeeded by another Italian, Carlo Vigarani, who was responsible for the decor of all the major fêtes at Versailles from *Les Plaisirs de l'Ile Enchantée* (1664), that included a comedy-ballet, *La Princesse d'Elide*, to *Le Triomphe de l'Amour* (1681) danced at Saint Germain and which was the swan-song of Louis XIV's court festivals.

Neither Torelli nor Vigarani, however, were responsible for the costumes which were the work of a series of French designers, much of whose work remains to be disentangled. The first of these was Henri de Beaubrun, court pastellist and *valet de la Garde-robe* who, according to Guillot de Saint Georges, introduced 'plusieurs nouveautés ingenieuses et galantes' in his contribution to

Le Ballet des Fées des Forêts de Saint Germain 1625. Grand Ballet. *Bibliothèque Nationale (right)*

Le Ballet des Fêtes de Bacchus 1651. Autumn. Studio of Gissey. *Bibliothèque Nationale (below left)*

Le Ballet des Fêtes de Bacchus 1651. Phantom. Studio of Gissey. *Bibliothèque Nationale*

Le Ballet des Fêtes de Bacchus. The second was Henri de Gissey, who designed more than a hundred dresses for *Le Ballet de la Nuit* and was responsible for the costumes for the famous horse-ballet or carrousel of 1662. He occupied the post of *Dessinateur de la chambre et du Cabinet du Roi* from 1660 to 1673. A series of his original annotated designs exist in the Bibliothèque Nationale and the Victoria & Albert Museum for ballets in the 1660s revealing him as an immensely capable draughtsman with a vigorous style in pen and wash. His work in the 1650s is known from studio copies of feeble aesthetic quality in the main, although capturing the very real variety and imagination of his work. His successor was Jean Berain who started designing costumes for Vigarani but subsequently took on the execution of both scenery and costumes. Berain's designs for ballet costumes were to gain a European currency through the engravings of Bonnart. There is an elegance and sophistication to them. They shed the

Henri de Gissey, costume for an entrée of ducks. *Department of Prints and Drawings, V & A (right)*
Henri de Gissey, costume for a dancer in a *ballet de cour*, c. 1660–70. *Department of Prints and Drawings, V & A (below left)*
Henri de Gissey, costume for a dancer in a *ballet de cour*, c. 1660–70. *Department of Prints and Drawings, V & A*

Le Triomphe de l'Amour 1681.
Costume for Mystery by Jean Berain.
Theatre Museum, V & A

heaviness of the baroque and anticipate the gaiety of the rococo. By the close of the century ballet had in fact shifted from the court to the public theatre in Paris. The era of the *ballet de cour* had reached its end and a new one was about to begin.

To the French *ballet de cour* at its height, however, we have a unique guide in Père Ménestrier's *Des Ballets Anciens et Modernes* (1681). In it he lays down rules governing costume in the ballet which he defines as four:

'The first condition is that the costume should be appropriate to the subject and, if the personage be historical, one should keep as far as possible to the costume of the period. That of the ancient Romans is the most dignified of all . . . The second condition is that the costumes should be greatly varied and, if possible, the same kind of dress should not appear twice . . . The third condition is that uniformity should be maintained as far as possible in the same entrées, that is to say, all those taking part in them should be dressed in the same colour and style if the subject permit . . . The fourth condition is that the costume shall not be cumbersome and shall leave the legs and body quite free to dance. The women's costumes are the least suitable because they must be long'.

Although ballet was to remain an ingredient of court festivals at Versailles down to the French Revolution the *ballet de cour* had passed its apogée and the initiatives that were to lead ultimately to the Romantic Ballet were to come from elsewhere.

The Stuart Court Masques

Across the Channel the same elements that in France had produced the *ballet de cour* led to the formation of quite a different kind of choreographic art, that of the court masque. Although the masque with its geometric choreographed dances was a form developed at the Elizabethan court, particularly during the 1590s, it was not until the advent of the Stuarts that it emerged as a definable form with the famous collaboration of Ben Jonson and Inigo Jones in the *Masque of Blackness* of 1605. In this Jones introduced for the first time some of the scenic effects used by the Italians. A curtain fell revealing a perspective seascape and the Queen and her ladies appeared as the Daughters of Niger in a maritime chariot drawn by sea monsters that floated on the waters. In the design for the costumes of the masquers, among the famous series preserved at Chatsworth covering the whole of Jones's creativity in the theatre down to 1640, what we see is still fundamentally an Elizabethan figure. Nonetheless this drawing is the earliest evidence we have of what dance costume was like within the masque tradition. In the first place the farthingale was obviously abandoned, and in this anticipated developments in fashion. The skirt was worn short to facilitate movement, a

curtailment that could lead to comment, and the main silhouette was always a variant on that of contemporary dress. Even though Jones has based his costume on that of an Aethiopian in Vecellio's book, the looped mantle echoes exactly the so-called Hibernian mantle that was the rage of fashionable dress of the period. And, as at the French court, the masquers were in the main dressed alike, except for the Queen who would usually be provided with an especially elaborate headdress. *Blackness* was a neoplatonic allegory on the power of kingship and the Queen and her ladies descended from their chariot, performed their ballet and after took out partners from the onlookers for the general courtly dancing known as the revels.

This basic format established in 1605 was to last forty years until it vanished with the outbreak of the Civil War. Its motivating force was overtly political for in the masques king and court, in the guise of virtues, heroes and heroines vanquished the opposition. They were staged almost without exception as Twelfth Night Revels or to mark a royal or aristocratic marriage. Jones wrote that the masques were 'nothing else but pictures with light and motion' and indeed in his view what he presented the court with was a glass in which they could view their platonic ideals. What he put on stage was a series of emblematic tableaux, the progression of which was always the same, either moving from disorder to order, or from order to disorder back to order again. And this was expressed for example by a storm scene being transformed into a garden, or a fiery hell into an ordered piazza.

All the scenery designs, therefore fall into two categories: scenes representing untamed nature – tempests, stormy seas, hellmouths, dark forests and mountains – and those implying earthly and heavenly harmony – calm havens, elegant villas, gardens, piazzas and palaces in the classical style together with cosmic visions of the stars and heavens in the form of tremendous cloud borne apparitions. And the costumes duplicate this. There are the costumes of those who facilitate the plot, the actors and singers, those of the musicians, all of whom are attired to complement the two main categories; those of the anti-masquers, the 'opposition' – witches, sick lovers, old-fashioned courtiers, puritans, quacks, and mountebanks – and of the masquers, personified by royal and noble persons revealed in tableau at the climax and lit down into the dancing area by escorting pages bearing torches. Their dresses always had to be glittering and revelatory to emphasise their role as heaven come down to earth.

Inigo Jones, in his role as the Vitruvian architect-engineer, was the presiding genius for four decades over every aspect of the visual side of these productions. Even before 1631, when he finally broke with Jonson, his descriptions of both scenery and costumes, were some-

The Masque of Blackness
1605. Inigo Jones, design
for the daughter of night.
Devonshire Collection,
Chatsworth

Hercule e Amore 1640. The Ballet of the Cupids. *Biblioteca Nazionale, Turin*

Dono del Re del Alpi a Madama Reale 1645. Entry of the inhabitants of Nice. *Biblioteca Nazionale, Turin*

Attributed to Gissey. Design for a dancer in a *ballet de cour*, 1650–60. *Department of Prints and Drawings, V & A*

I1 Gridelino 1653. Ballet of the Ladies devoted to the colour 'gris de lin'. *Biblioteca Nazionale, Turin*

I1 Falso Amor Bandito, L'Humano Amisso et I1 Celeste Esaltato 1667. *Biblioteca Nazionale, Turin*

times printed as part of the published masque texts. After 1631 his control was total and it was Jones, in consultation with Charles I, who chose the plots and allegories of the masques, employing various poets to articulate them in words. Parallel with developments at the French court the masque setting gradually changed. England was in fact initially far in advance of France. By 1611 Jones had already ceased to use the turning machine or *machina versatilis* and adopted the use of side wings and shutters, the *scena ductalis*, which gave him flexibility to achieve any number of scene changes. By the early 1630s he had abandoned square *proscenia* in favour of rectangular ones, thus enabling the curtain to rise for the first time and opening the way for the development of the fly gallery for elaborate ascents and descents. Up until 1638 the masque theatres had all been temporary, inserted into the Whitehall Banqueting House, but in that year a wooden masquing room was erected, forerunner of what would have been a permanent court theatre at Whitehall on the lines of the *salle des machines* at the Tuileries.

Costume for Jones was always integrated into the overall Platonism of the masque visions. In his account of Henrietta Maria as Divine Beauty in *Tempe Restored* (1632) he follows his description of her dress by saying that he had designed it 'so that corporeal beauty, consisting in symmetry, colour, and certain inexpressible graces, shining in the Queen's Majesty, may draw us to a contemplation of the beauty of the soul, unto which it hath an analogy'. Dress for Jones in the masques was never merely splendid decoration or an interpretation of character but in itself a vehicle for morals and philosophy. To a Platonist such as Jones, truths were best expressed by images and the masque costumes were, together with the scenery, potent evidence of his belief in the power of conceptualized abstractions, of emblems and hieroglyphs as vehicles revealing hidden truth. For the renaissance mind whether the audience immediately understood the allusions in a costume or not was irrelevant. They enjoyed contemplating 'remov'd mysteries' and understanding could follow later. Jonson later jibes at Jones over this:

> Attire the persons as no thought can teach
> Sense what they are.

Jones actually could ignore Jonson's directions as to attribute, although he relied on exactly the same type of manual to compile them. Ripa's *Iconologia* was one of his greatest quarries, used selectively and totally idiosyncratically. Originality did not concern him and, as in the case of scenery, his borrowing from engraved sources is all but literal. Of these, the work of Jacques Callot proved to be a perpetual inspiration for anti-masque characters during the 1630s.

Dance played an important role as the climax of the masques, prefacing and intermingling the general court dancing in which masquers and courtiers took part. The same philosophical context was behind these dances as those in the *ballet de cour*, dance as a reflection of the cosmos, but we have no evidence that the figures were hieroglyphical on any scale as they could be in the French ballet where, for example, in 1610 the dancers performed the druid's alphabet. On the other hand evidence points to the fact that both Jonson and Jones regarded the choreography as an extension of the symbolic content

Tethys' Festival 1610. Inigo Jones, Tethys or a River Nymph. *Devonshire Collection, Chatsworth*

and must have worked hand in hand with the dancing masters. In *Hymenaei* (1606) the ceremony of an antique wedding was interrupted by an anti-masque dance in which the four humours and affections upset its progress to 'a kind of contentious music'. Order, as Reason's servant, presented the main masque as a dance expressing 'the harmonious laws of Nature and Reason'. The figures, Jonson tells us, were firstly letters 'very signifying

Lord's Masque 1613. Inigo Jones, A Transformed Statue, Lady Masquer. *Devonshire Collection, Chatsworth (left)*

Lord's Masque 1613. Inigo Jones, Masquer: A Star. *Devonshire Collection, Chatsworth*

to the bridegroom' followed by linking hands in a chain as an image of 'the golden chain let down from heaven'. At the close they were cast into 'a fair orb or circle' with Reason at its centre expounding on its allegorical significance. The lady masquers came as the Powers of Juno, their costumes 'after some statues of Juno'. The latter would be extremely difficult to reconcile with the three portraits that survive of these grand ladies wearing dresses which, far from evoking classical statues, remain squarely fancified versions of contemporary court dress with short skirts revealing a shoe with a slight heel. Face masks also would have been obligatory.

Three years later in the *Masque of Queens* (1609) the contrast of the dances became an established ingredient

with the introduction of an anti-masque of witches who executed 'a magical dance full of preposterous change and gesticulation'. The twelve queens danced one figure which was the name of Charles, Duke of York. In *Love Restored* (1612) the dance represented the order of the virtues, in *The Golden Age Restored* (1615) that of the Golden Age, in *Tethys Festival* (1610) the queen and her ladies serpentined their way across the dancing arena in a way appropriate to the rivers they personified. The costumes incorporated headdresses 'composed of shells and coral' and a dress adorned 'with maritime invention'.

In the Jacobean phase down to 1625 there is no great change in the main masque and its dances that we know of but there was a marked development in the anti-masque both in number and in use of dance and mime. The implication is that these were nearly always executed by professionals. In *Pleasure Reconciled to Virtue* (1618) there was one of men dressed as bottles and a cask and another of pigmies. In the *Masque of Augurs* (1622) one anti-masque was 'a perplexed dance of straying and deformed pilgrims'. The designs that survive for these indicate Jones's skill for comic dress. From 1615 onwards all the masques were male led by Charles I as Prince of Wales. The drawings for men's costumes are *à l'antique*

For the Honour of Wales 1618. Inigo Jones, Anti-Masque of Welsh Dancers. *Devonshire Collection, Chatsworth*

with elements of contemporary dress and a touch of the exotic. Elaborate feathered headdresses were the norm, and cloaks which were removed for the dancing.

The masques of the years of Charles I's personal rule during the 1630s form a final distinctive phase. Their preoccupation without exception was with the exultation of the monarchy, in which King and Queen adopt the identity of their Platonic ideals in a series of startling epiphanies. In these Charles presented himself as heroic lover, priest, king and, finally in the last of the masques, *Salmacida Spolia* (1640), as a ruler whose perfection had gone unrecognised by his own people and whose attributes were now those of Christ betrayed. Under the impact of a French Queen, Henrietta Maria, there was a vast multiplication of anti-masques which now approximated closely to the French *ballet à entrées* on which she had been brought up. There is, however, nothing in Jones's costumes that approaches the fantasies of Rabel,

although there was clearly a vast development in mime and dance characterisation from *Love's Triumph through Callipolis* (1631) onwards. In that masque, which opened the series of the years of Personal Rule, depraved lovers danced 'a distracted comedy of love, expressing their confused affections in the scenical persons and habits of the four prime European nations' ending in a circle to express a submission to order. Three years later in *Coelum Britanicum* (1634) the anti-masques must have been even more highly developed. In one instance the star signs that embodied the vices descended from a starry sphere

> Clad in those proper figures by which best
> Their incorporeal nature is expressed.

These emblematic figures danced 'expressing the deviation from virtue'. By 1640 in the last masque these *entrées* had multiplied to as many as twenty. In the characters chosen the whole spectrum of the opponents of Charles's rule was anatomised: 'antique cavaliers', rosicrucians, 'roaring boys', 'mad lovers', and an 'old-fashioned Englishman and his mistress'. Unlike the designs for the main masquers in those for his anti-masque characters Jones is thinking the whole time in terms of movement of the most lively kind.

Vast masses of his designs are not for dancers at all but for the actors, singers and musicians who facilitated the progress of the plot. There are also ones for the torchbearers, who sometimes danced, but whose main function was to provide an escort for the descent of the masquers from the stage to the arena and illumine their dances. The sets in contrast were lit by candles placed behind bowls filled by different coloured waters. Lighting explains the relatively restricted range of colours chosen for the masquers costumes, which were almost invariably *en suite* and the favourite colours were white, carnation, watchet and green with an abundant use of spangles, and gold and silver lace to catch the light. And no expense was spared in respect of the richness of fabric and materials.

Throughout the 1630s masque dress continued to approximate to court dress, reflecting the subdued elegance of the Caroline age immortalised in Van Dyck's portraits. Jones went to enormous trouble over the royal costumes and whole sets of preliminary and alternative designs were prepared for submission to both the king and queen. The masque texts, with Jonson out of the way, provide greater detail about the costumes and much significance was attached to them. 'The description of the several habits of the main masque, anti-masques, with all

Time Vindicated 1620. Inigo Jones, The Eyed, the Eared and the Nosed. *Devonshire Collection, Chatsworth*

Chloridia 1631. Inigo Jones, costume for Henrietta Maria. *Devonshire Collection, Chatsworth (right)*

This desseigne I conceaue to bee fitt for the inuention and if it pleas hir Ma.^ts
to add or alter any thing I desire to receaue hir Ma.^ts comaund and tho.
desseigne againe by this bearer.   the collors allso are in hir Ma.^ts
choise; but my oppinion is that seuerall fresh greenes mix with gould and
siluer will be most propper

98.

Britannia Triumphans 1938. Inigo Jones, preliminary sketches for the Anti-Masquers. *Devonshire Collection, Chatsworth*

the people employed', Jones writes in *Tempe Restored* (1632) 'would make a book alone as big as this'. Choreographically, however, we know little. In *Love's Triumph* (1631) the perfect lovers ranged themselves in a 'circle of the will' and focussed their attention on the King who stood in the middle personifying Heroic Love. Subsequent texts tell us virtually nothing, although it is clear that to the very end the masque dance always expressed love, virtue and order, an image of harmony, of the King's Peace, and through that a glimpse of a higher harmony, and a deeper wisdom. Absolutism in France was to ensure that the *ballet de cour* was to reach its peak as an art form. The Civil War in England precluded the

Coelum Britannicum, 1634. Inigo Jones, A Masquer as an Ancient Hero. *Devonshire Collection, Chatsworth*

development of the court masque into a form we would more readily recognise as an antecedent of our modern ballet. That was its tragedy.

The *ballet de cour* in Savoy

The Stuart court masques were a unique development. On the mainland ballet became an export of the French court. The marriage of Henry IV's sister, Catherine, in 1599 to the son of Duke Charles III took the art to the court of Lorraine: She had organised ballets in the darkest days of the French wars of religion at the tiny court over which she presided at Pau. In 1600 the first ballet was danced at Nancy, the ladies entering on a chariot like a garden from which they descended to dance. Six years later there was an even more spectacular ballet on the occasion of the marriage festivals of Henry of Lorraine to Margherita Gonzaga. This time the dancers came as twelve goddesses led in by Cupid. In 1638 the ballet was imported to Sweden from France by Oxenstierna. By 1645 perspective sets were in use and subsequently a French machinist was imported to erect a permanent *salle des fêtes*. Réné Descartes was ordered by Queen Christina to devise a ballet to celebrate the Peace of Munster. *Le Ballet de la naissance de la Paix* (1649) glorified eternal wisdom in the form of Pallas (Christina) and paraded a series of *entrées* in which pillagers, ruined peasantry and mocking soldiers danced the horrors of the Thirty Years War.

There was one court, however, that deserves more detailed mention, that of the Dukes of Savoy. In 1619 Henry IV's daughter, Christina, Madame Royale, married Victor Amadeus, heir to Duke Charles Emmanuel I. Savoy geographically formed a bridgehead between France and Italy and the court at Turin was one of the most splendid in Europe as the warlike dukes cultivated in particular all forms of chivalrous festival with a carrousel tradition vigorous until the close of the 17th century. The arrival of Christina quickly established the *ballet de cour* at the centre of festival forms at the Savoy court for the next forty five years until her death in 1663. In this she was aided by the presiding genius of Count Filippo d'Aglié who devised virtually every court entertainment for nearly four decades until his demise four years after his mistress in 1667. Père Ménestrier describes Aglié as a 'Chevalier accompli . . . versé dans les connaissances de l'Histoire, de l'Antiquité, de la Politique et de toutes les belles lettres, (il) composoit excellement en Vers Latins, Italiens et Francais, jouoit de toutes sortes d'Instrumens, composoit en Musique'. Aglié not only conceived the plots and allegories of the ballets but supervised the scenery and costumes and directed the performances as a whole. He was also a brilliant choreographer who, according to the poet Tesauro, believed ballet was 'an acting metaphor, signifying by means of gesture and movement, the interior affections, and the exterior actions of man'. As one of the ducal secretaries of state he was close to political events so that the ballets were always, to use Ménestrier words again, 'Allegories de l'Estat des temps'.

Their importance is heightened because of a unique visual record, unrivalled elsewhere, of the appearance of these court festivals. Thirteen volumes covering the years 1640 to 1681 preserved in the Biblioteca Reale and the Biblioteca Nazionale di Torino were compiled by and under the aegis of one of the ducal secretaries, Tommaso Borgonio. These evoke vividly every detail of the performances. They are not designs but rather a record of almost archaeological exactness.

Ballets were presented at court on the Duke's and Madame Royale's birthdays, at Carnival time and on S. Nicola's day. Aglié's first ballet was *Prometeo che rubba il fuoco* (1627) and eleven more followed down to 1640. For these we have texts but no illustrations. The latter begin in that year with *Hercole e Amore* and eleven more ballets follow down to his death. As in the case of the Stuart court masques they are heavily political and deal in allegorical form with the difficulties of the Duchy of Savoy under the regency of Christina as she endeavoured to preserve its independence against the might of both France and Spain.

The illustrations tell us that already by 1640 baroque staging was well established with its use of side wings and back shutters to facilitate change and machinery for ascents and descents. Only after 1650 was the influence of Torelli to lead to an even greater emphasis on scenic spectacle. *L'Educatione di Achille e delle Nereidi* (1650) had no less than seven changes as against the three in *Hercole e Amore* ten years before.

Costume in the Savoy ballets reflected exactly a court placed between France and a Spanish dominated peninsula. The ladies in *Il Gridelino* (1653) wear a fanciful version of Habsburg court dress onto which are added vaguely antique details with a veil floating from a coronet. Throughout, male costume betrays its tiltyard origins with towering feathered headdress and a skirt derived from the bases worn over armour. This was to develop into the *tonnelet* of the next century. The shoes have a slight heel but in the case of the men there was little in their attire to impede movement. But the real fascination of these volumes lies in the fantastic and comic *entrées* costumes. Although a direct French importation they are closer in mood to those in the Caroline masques and, we must remember, Madame Royale was Henrietta Maria's sister. These range over the whole conspectus of subject matter suitable to Savoy. Tobacco-smoking Spaniards are a vehicle for satire on the enemy in *Il Tobacco* (1650) and are dressed in a caricature of Spanish costume. In *Il Dono del Re del Alpi* (1645) the *entrées* are of dancers in regional costumes in homage to Madame Royale. In *L'Unione per la peregrina Margherita*

Reale e Celeste (1660) the *entrées* embark on an eastern exoticism in tribute to the pearl (Margherita of Savoy) beyond price whose marriage to the Duke of Parma this ballet celebrated.

By *L'Unione* the ballet element was balanced by an equal amount of acting and singing. The *entrées* were also more closely integrated into the overall plot and the ballet was divided into separate acts. But the ballet tradition, although dwindling, was so strong that when the opera *Lisamaco* (1681) was performed as part of the Carnival of 1681 nine *entrées* had to be inserted. But the golden age was over.

The decline of the *ballet de cour*

By the 1680s all over Europe the *ballet de cour* had passed its zenith. Like other forms of festival born in the renaissance its thought context had begun to vanish. Its images depended on a philosophy that seeing was believing. It was a true off-spring of the renaissance hermetic tradition in which mysteries and truths were wrapped in symbols and arcane images. The *ballet de cour* belonged firmly to this world of correspondences in which dance was a mirror of the ordered movement of an earth-centred cosmos. Once the vision of man the microcosm was shattered and the age of magic gave way to that of science and enlightenment, the *ballet de cour* was doomed. Ballet dress in that world had in one of its aspects the aim to make manifest to the audience the realm of the Platonic idea. The vast sums lavished on the decor and costumes of these transitory spectacles are testimony enough to princely faith in their power and efficacy. In the Age of Reason that followed such potent hieroglyphic visions, which is how the artists and designers of the age of absolutism had seen them, became merely scenery and costumes as ballet ceased to be ritual confined to the court and became merely entertainment in a public theatre performed by professionals.

Select bibliography

The following works all contain extensive bibliographies:
Marie-Françoise Christout, *Le Ballet de Cour de Louis XIV (1643–72)*, Vie Musicale en France sous les Rois Bourbons, 12, Paris, 1967.
Mercedes Viale Ferrero, *Feste delle Madame Reali di Savoia*, Turin 1965.
Margaret McGowan, *L'art du Ballet de Cour en France 1581–1643*, CNRS, Paris, 1963.
Margaret McGowan, 'Les fêtes de cour en Savoie. L'Oeuvre du Philippe d'Aglié', *Révue d'Historie du Théâtre*, III, 1970.
Stephen Orgel and Roy Strong, *Inigo Jones. The Theatre of the Stuart Court*, London, 1973.
Henry Prunières, *Le Ballet de Cour en France avant Benserade et Lully*, Paris, 1914.
Frances A. Yates, *The Valois Tapestries*, London, 1959

Costume and the Nineteenth Century Dancer

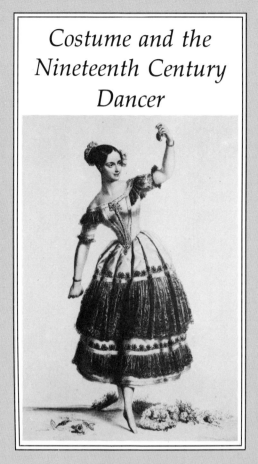

IVOR GUEST

Aside from its function to entertain, the theatre exists as a projection of man's fantasies, and the costumes of the players – be they actors, singers or dancers – reflect, inevitably, the styles and fashions of the passing years, not merely because those who design them are conditioned by what they see around them, but also because the spectators are thereby better enabled to relate to the action on the stage. In the case of a drama on a contemporary theme such a statement is obvious, but it is less so in the more artificial theatrical form of ballet. Because of its independence from speech, ballet has always been an exceptionally potent medium for conveying fantasy and mood, since the body is capable of expression through its own movement. In the receptive process of the spectator of ballet it is the eye that plays the dominant role, and the visual effect of the movement, whether dance or mime, is always influenced by the style and colour of the costumes, which, if designed with inspiration, can become an extension of the dancer's body and personality.

The designer of costumes for the ballet was not to be fully recognised as an artist in his own right until the twentieth century, but long before then many talented hands had applied their pencils, pens and brushes to devising costumes for the productions that became the foundations on which ballet was eventually to emerge as a mature and major art.

The eighteenth century was a period of momentous development. When it opened an old and care-worn Louis XIV sat on the throne of France, and only some of the older courtiers could remember the great *ballets de cour* of his youth. While the dance traditions that had been developed in those magnificent entertainments flourished no longer at court, they had sturdily taken root in the theatre when the Paris Opéra had been established. In his operas that made up its early repertory, Lully had preserved the *ballet de cour*'s basic concept of a composite form, in which the dance was an important and essential element. He no less appreciated the importance of spectacle, and made an inspired choice of designer. Jean Bérain was an exceptionally inventive artist whose costume sketches were conceived in a graceful baroque idiom that was ideally suited to the *noble* style of dancing as it was then practised. Basing them on contemporary court dress, he skilfully made adjustments to permit greater liberty of movement, leaving the male dancer's legs free to perform the expansive steps required of him and shortening the skirts of the women, whose dancing was less demanding, just enough in the front to allow the feet to be perceived. In contrast to these stately costumes,

Bérain revealed an extraordinarily fertile imagination in his designs for character dancers and for fantastic beings such as furies, winds and demons, introducing a rich variety of colour and texture that left a strong personal stamp on the productions of his time.

The death of the old king in 1715 ushered in a less solemn age, in which the dance attained even greater prominence at the Opéra. As dancers' technique became more complex and spectacular, lighter material was used in the making of their costumes. The introduction of the farthingale in feminine fashion led naturally to the adoption of a bell-shaped ankle-length skirt of a form that

Marie Thérèse de Subligny, one of the first ballerinas of the Paris Opéra costumed for dance in the noble style. *Department of Prints and Drawings, V & A*

appeared in the designs of Claude Gillot for the ballet *Les Eléments* in 1721. A few years later the skirt was shortened a few inches more to display the sparkling *entrechats* of Camargo. By 1730 the silhouette of the ballerina's costume attained a degree of near perfection which was to influence design for some fifty years and was immortalised in Lancret's celebrated painting of Camargo in action. On a more intimate level the animated movements that women were being called upon to perform necessitated another innovation that was less apparent to the spectator – the wearing of close-fitting drawers that were descriptively known as *caleçons de précaution*.

To modern eyes, the male dancer of the eighteenth century appears less well served by the costumier. Perhaps this was due to the concept of the *danse noble*, a

Jean Balon dressed for a noble dance. *Bibliothèque Nationale*

(left)

Henri Dumoulin in character dance, Paris Opéra c. 1700. *Department of Prints and Drawings, V & A*

very abstract form of dancing which had a definite meaning to the aristocratic audience of the eighteenth century, harking back to the apogée of Louis XIV's glory and perpetuating the image of the Sun King in a way that was becoming more and more corrupted through being performed no longer by a courtier but by a professional dancer. Casanova's memoirs contain a vivid description of Louis Dupré dancing with immense dignity in a black wig reaching half way down his back and an open coat that fell almost to his heels, but the more usual costume of the *danseur noble*, which was still being worn in Paris in the 1760s, incorporated the curious item of clothing known as the *tonnelet*, a padded kilt-like appendage covering the thighs and at times spreading out to a ridiculous width like an abbreviated *panier*.

During the eighteenth century the task of designing the costumes of the Paris Opéra passed through the hands of a succession of artists – Claude Gillot, François Boucher, Jean-Baptiste Martin, Louis-René Boquet – who set fashions that were followed in opera houses throughout Europe. Viewed chronologically, their designs reveal a

Costume design by Louis-René Bouquet for Jean Dauberval and Mlle. Peslin. *Bibliothèque Nationale*

Costume design by Louis-René Bouquet for Gaetan Vestris. *Bibliothèque Nationale* (right)

progressive trend towards a rococo artificiality which may have added charm to the diverting interludes in operas for which they were designed, but were to prove inappropriate for the more realistic demands of the *ballet d'action*.

The introduction and eventual acceptance of this novel form of spectacle was to give ballet an identity of its own, and make it independent of the opera, in which it had formerly been incorporated. Mainly this was achieved by the use of pantomime to express the action, but at the same time it was necessary to sweep away a number of artificial conventions, not least in the area of costume, to produce a more natural and meaningful effect. The impetus for this momentous development came not from Paris, but from Vienna, Milan and Stuttgart where Hilverding, Noverre and Angiolini found the conditions they required to put their theories in practice. To these innovators the Paris Opéra was a stronghold of reaction, and in his *Letters sur la Danse et les Ballets*, published in 1760, Noverre called for reform, specifying in particular the changes that were needed in ballet costume: the abolition of the *tonnelet* and also of the mask, which had long since ceased to serve a useful purpose, and the reduction of the width of the *paniers* worn by female dancers.

There was a world of difference between the highly refined ballet of the old school and the ideals of these progressive ballet-masters. The incongruous appearance

Jason et Medée. King's Theatre, with Vestris, Baccelli, and Simonet. *Department of Prints and Drawings, V & A*

of the conventional ballet costumes of the mid-century in the context of a *ballet d'action* was clearly demonstrated in a drawing of a ballet on a Pygmalion theme, possibly by Hilverding, made around 1750. Thirty years later, when the *ballet d'action* was taking root, the costume designers still had not completely discarded the hidebound conventions that exasperated Noverre. In John Boydell's satirical engraving of a mime scene in *Médée et Jason* at the King's Theatre, London in 1781, the expressive acting of the performers is vividly portrayed, but their costumes bear no relationship to the action.

The costume conventions against which Noverre fulminated were applied less rigidly to the *demi-caractère* and *comique* styles of dancing, and as his designs reveal,

JASON ET MEDEE   BALLET TRAGIQUE.

Auguste Vestris, the proponent of the demi-caractère style.
Department of Prints and Drawings, V & A

Boquet allowed himself considerably more freedom when designing for dancers such as Lany and Dauberval, but the Opéra never descended to the raw realism that enlivened the unpretentious ballets at the Comédie-Italienne at the middle of the century. Modestly foreshadowing the light bucolic ballets of Noverre and Dauberval, they presented scenes from contemporary life, full of boisterous comedy and performed in ordinary everyday costumes, and exuded a crude but spontaneous vitality that was singularly lacking at the Opéra.

By the 1780s, when the *ballet d'action* was firmly established on every great opera house stage, even in Paris, a fundamental change of artistic taste was taking place. The rococo style, with its mannered and artificial graces, was passing out of favour and being replaced by the austere forms of neoclassicism. The neoclassical concept that art should aspire to imitate nature was adopted not only by the choreographers of the late eighteenth century, but also by their costume designers, who began to dress the dancers in a natural fashion that presented them as rec-

ognisable characters from real life instead of over-dressed animated dolls.

This new wave of ballet, for such it was, found its most sensitive exponent in Jean Dauberval, whose works, to quote a phrase of the time, 'spoke to the heart' and were to be regarded as models well into the succeeding century. The most celebrated of these was a trifle which he threw off on the eve of the French Revolution, in July 1789, *La Fille mal gardée*. Its significance lay in it being not an artificial pastorale appealing to sentimental tastes but a timeless little comedy whose characters were ordinary country-folk, a widow and her mischievous daughter, the boy with whom the girl is in love, and a wealthy farmer whose simple-minded son the widow sees as her future son-in-law. These familiar figures were presented in costumes that added an authentic touch to the situations of the ballet.

Dauberval would doubtless be surprised, perhaps even a little upset, to know that the twentieth century was to remember him by this slight work, and not by one of his more substantial productions, such as his 'anacreontic' ballet, *Télémaque* (1791). This was the form which his contemporary Pierre Gardel exploited with such conspicuous success at the Paris Opéra around the turn of the

The Church protests at the indecency of dancers' costumes at the King's Theatre, London. *Theatre Museum, V & A*

century. Gardel's *Télémaque* (1790), *Psyché* (1790) and *Le Jugement de Pâris* (1793), which became the mainstay of the French repertory for some forty years, were entirely neoclassical in intention and effect. Visually they were motivated by the same spirit that inspired the paintings of Jacques-Louis David and his school, and to this end the style of the costumes, simple in cut and revealing the lines and curves of the dancers' bodies, played a most significant part. Not only were these costumes singularly appropriate for characters out of classical mythology, but for the first time they revealed the whole body, undistorted by artificial accessories such as corsets, hoops and *tonnelets*, and the dancers' skills could be displayed to full advantage at the very moment that important technical developments were being introduced.

These costumes naturally reflected the fashions of the day. As if in reaction to the nightmare of the Terror, the ladies of Paris had begun to appear in the flimsiest of dresses in deference to the 'classical' taste of the time. Corsets and petticoats were discarded, and the lightest of materials were used so that the dresses clung seductively to the body. Notwithstanding that Europe was at war, Paris fashions were soon copied elsewhere, and what was acceptable in society was equally permissible on the stage. There was no lack of self-appointed guardians of public morals to inveigh against the shameless appearance of female ballet dancers, and the display of their bodies was one of the factors that was to place them beyond the pale of respectable society until the twentieth century. In 1798 the Bishop of Durham, in a somewhat intemperate speech in the House of Lords, attacked the indecent attitudes of the French dancers who were appearing at the King's Theatre. Journalists and caricaturists lost no time in making fun of the unfortunate prelate, but the opera house authorities nevertheless considered it prudent to turn their attention to the costumes of the female dancers, and orders were given that the flesh-coloured stockings used hitherto were to be replaced by white stockings.

The male dancers incurred no such odium, although their costumes too had become simpler and more natural. Men had always been allowed to show off their shapely legs and the disappearance of the *tonnelet*, the padded skirt worn by *danseurs nobles* in the mid-eighteenth century, had given them greater freedom of movement well before 1800. By that year the *demi-caractère* style of dancing, which combined a less affected manner with the display of brilliant technique, had become predominant, and its principal exponents, Auguste Vestris and Louis Duport, appeared before the public clad more simply, as the taste of the time demanded. Basically their costume consisted of a tunic or jacket reaching to the mid-thigh, knee-breeches and stockings, but if the ballet had an anacreontic subject, their legs were sometimes apparently unstockinged and bare.

Viewed in relation to the development of choreography and execution, this simplification of costume was immensely and lastingly beneficial, for it not only liberated the body so that it could respond to the demands of a rapidly improving dance technique but also, by revealing so much of it to the spectator, reduced the opportunities for concealing technical shortcomings in performance. Most of all, this liberation added a new dimension to the female dancer's art. She now found herself free of the ground, able to soar into the air and also to lift her body upwards, reducing the area of contact with the floor more and more until she was touching it with the mere tips of her toes or, to use the term that later came into appearance, the *pointes*. The introduction of the heel-less shoe

The trend towards simplicity in the 1790s. Mlle. Parisot, a French dancer popular in London. *Theatre Museum, V & A*

towards the end of the eighteenth century had made this important innovation possible. At its inception around the turn of the century it entered the ballerina's vocabulary unnoticed, being limited at first to mere momentary risings. It was not generally remarked until Geneviève Gosselin began to exploit it in about 1810, although there were undoubtedly ballerinas before her who had achieved the feat.

Neoclassicism, with its preoccupation with the grandeur of the Roman Empire, was losing its force when Napoleon was finally defeated at Waterloo in 1815. When Europe found itself at peace after twenty-five years of war, great changes had taken place. With the emergence of a strong middle class and the expansion of industry, new political ideas and social attitudes were emerging, and in the realms of art a younger generation of artists was turning its back on the forms and conventions of the previous century and, following the instinct of their feelings, evolving trends that were to crystallise into the

Neoclassicism as expressed in the anacreontic ballet. Two celebrated French dancers, Louis Duport and Auguste Vestris. *Theatre Museum, V & A*

Romantic movement. In Austria the Biedermeier style made its appearance, with its unpretentious simplicity and its emphasis on family virtue, a cosy style which was a conscious reaction against the flamboyance and licence of the early years of the century and was to lead to the more ponderous forms that were to dominate Victorian England, Second Empire France and the Vienna of Hans Makart.

After Waterloo feminine fashion underwent a rapid change. The waist, which had risen high under the bosom during the Empire, dropped to a more natural level, the corset was readopted, the 'leg of mutton' sleeve emphasised the width of the shoulders and the skirt became wider and fuller. All this produced a very different silhouette, less natural than during the dominance of neoclassical lines, but idealising the feminine figure by emphasising those characteristics which distinguished it from the male – the bust, the waist, the hips – and at the same time, by adding to the weight and circumference of the skirt, proclaiming her inviolability. These trends were to last well into the next century, for the female body was not to be liberated again from the imprisoning restrictions of dress until after the First World War.

Stage costume continued to be directly influenced by fashion, and designers working for the ballet echoed the styles in vogue. Ballet, in the early nineteenth century, was considered to be an essentially French form of art, just as opera was then regarded as Italian, and the Paris Opéra's supremacy in this field was not seriously challenged until the last decades of the century.

At the Paris Opéra the costume designer was an employee, invested with the responsibility of dressing the singers and dancers in every opera and ballet production, but very definitely regarded as inferior in status to the other creative artists – the musician and the choreographer, the librettist and the designer of the scenery, all of whom, unlike the costume designer, enjoyed the satisfaction of hearing their names announced from the stage at the conclusion of a first performance. For all that, the costume designers were men of undeniable professional skill, and sometimes excelled in other branches of painting.

During the Republic and the First Empire Jean-Simon Barthélémy costumed Pierre Gardel's major ballets in the neoclassical style, dressing gods in simple tunics and goddesses in diaphanous chitons for the anacreontic scenes so popular at that time. By 1819, when Auguste Garneray was appointed to the post, there had been a significant change in taste and fashion. Garneray's designs reflected the trend towards heavier materials,

The elaboration of dancer's costumes in the 1820s. Albert (Francois Decombe) and Emilie Bigottini in a *pas de deux* from Aumer's *Cendrillon* (Paris Opéra, 1823). *Department of Prints and Drawings, V & A (right)*

with a lower waist and bouffant sleeves for the women, and typified the 'Renaissance troubadour' style that dominated the fashions of the 1820s. His costumes were notable for the elaborate decoration of the material, the stage jewellery which he devised with great attention to detail, and the plumes that both male and female dancers were constrained to wear. The shift of fashion that took

Auguste Garneray's costume design for a dancer in Spontini's opera *Olimpie* (Paris Opéra, 1819). *National Art Library, V & A*

place at this time is well illustrated by a comparison of some of the designs that span a period of only four years. That Garneray could work in the simpler neoclassical idiom is evident from an early design for an ethereal dancer's costume for Spontini's opera *Olimpie*, produced in 1819. Four years later, the costumes for Aumer's ballet *Cendrillon*, designed by the choreographer Albert, reveal new trends, particularly in the more lavish use of material and a fussy decoration that had its counterpart in the costumes for another, more pompous spectacle of the period – the coronation of Charles X at Rheims.

Garneray was succeeded, briefly, by Alexandre Fragonard, an artist of lesser stature than his celebrated father but held in sufficient regard to be given credit, most exceptionally, for his costumes for Deshayes' ballet *Zémire et Azor* (1824). He in turn was succeeded by Hippolyte Lecomte, a painter of historical subjects, who designed the ballets during the last few years of the Bourbon restoration, before the full impact of Romanticism was felt at the Opéra. Lecomte's elegant costumes were particularly flattering to the female figure. The ravishing Neapolitan costume he conceived for Lise Noblet, for example, in the mime role of Fenella in Auber's opera *La Muette de Portici* (1828) was chicly Parisian with its embroidered apron, the ribbons hanging from the corsage, the beribboned leg-of-mutton sleeves, and yet more ribbons in the hair, which was noticeably more simply styled than had been the fashion a few years earlier. As was to be expected from a historical painter, Lecomte's costumes for Aumer's ballet *Manon Lescaut* (1830) were designed with scholarly accuracy, but the design that strikes the eyes most forcefully today, is the one for the simple white dress worn by Pauline Montessu in the sleepwalking scene in *La Somnambule* in 1827, which prefigures the Romantic tutu.

A pronounced reaction had set in against the revealing fashions of a generation earlier. It was generally believed that the sensibilities of Charles X had been offended by the short and diaphanous costumes that ballerinas still favoured, and the Vicomte Sosthène de la Rochefoucauld, who as Superintendant of Theatres exercised supervisory powers at the Opéra, earned royal approval and a footnote in history by requiring their skirts to be longer and made of thicker material. This order aroused much ribald comment, but it was in tune with the more decorous trends that were beginning to influence feminine fashion.

At the Paris Opéra in the 1820s the costumes worn by the male dancers still gave an indication of the *genre* to which they belonged in the company's organisation. Every dancer was then classified as being *noble, demi-*

A pre-echo of the Romantic tutu. Pauline Montessu in the sleep-walking scene in Aumer's ballet *La Somnambule* (Paris Opéra, 1827). *Musée de l'Opéra, Paris (right)*

caractère or *comique*, according to his style and physique, even though the boundaries between these *genres* were becoming increasingly blurred. Particularly favoured by the *danseur noble* was a doublet, close-fitting round the torso but widening out below the waist to allow him freedom to perform the majestic steps that were his speciality – *développés*, attitudes and arabesques performed with a punctilious regard for their lines and correctness. The decoration of his doublet could be as elaborate as anything designed for the female dancer, and the costume was generally completed by some form of hat. If the ballet were of the anacreontic type, peopled with the

Above – the three genres of classical dancer distinguished by their costume: noble (Greek tunic), demi-caractère (Spanish troubadour), comique (villageois). Below – principal group from a ballet by Blasis. *Theatre Museum, V & A*

deities of Olympus or characters from mythology, the doublet might be replaced by a short chiton of light material, with little decoration, and perhaps attached at one shoulder, leaving the opposite side of the chest bare. The alternative fashion for male dancers was more suited to the *demi-caractère* and *comique* styles, which called especially for vigour, speed and precision. For these athletic virtuosos loose garments had to be avoided and the legs were encased in tight knee-breeches and stockings, the character of the role being conveyed in the style and decoration of the garment worn over the upper part of the body, such as an embroidered waistcoat or lederhosen with a long-sleeved shirt beneath. This style had been popular then for some years, and was to become the accepted uniform of the male dancer and the counterpart of the Romantic tutu.

To commission an outside designer for a specific work

would have been unthinkable at the Opéra and indeed at any other European opera house at that time, but there were one or two instances of independent artists being asked, or allowed, to contribute isolated sketches. The most distinguished of these was Eugène Delacroix, one of the greatest of Romantic painters, who designed a costume for his friend, François Simon, to wear in Aumer's *La Belle au bois dormant* (1829). More frequently to be met within the walls of the Opéra at that time was the watercolourist Eugène Lami, who was first charged with the task of designing military uniforms for *Manon Lescaut* (1830) and Coralli's *L'Orgie* (1831), and who then sketched a series of characteristic Scotsmen for a new ballet in preparation for Marie Taglioni.

La Sylphide (1832), as this work was called, proved to be one of the most significant landmarks in the history of ballet. The first purely Romantic ballet, it became the prototype of a spate of productions conceived around supernatural creatures, that flooded the opera houses of Europe not only while Romanticism retained its vital force but long afterwards. In outline its subject was deceptively uncomplicated – the appearance of a sylphide to disturb the love of a young Scotsman and his fiancée with tragic results for both hero and spirit – but it afforded unusual scope to the designers of both scenery and costumes. The two sets, and especially the forest scene for the second act, were among the finest creations of the great Ciceri, and Lami proved to be an inspired choice to dress the real-life characters in the kilts and plaids of the Scottish highlands. However, mystery has continued to surround the origin of the simple white costume that Taglioni and her attendant sylphides wore, for the designs that are preserved in the Library of the Paris Opéra comprise only three sketches by Lami of Scottish types, the all-important design for Taglioni's costume being missing.

It has been conjectured that Lami designed the costumes for the entire ballet, but Carlos Fischer, in the course of the research for his authoritative book, *Les Costumes de l'Opéra*, spoke with several members of Lami's family who remembered the painter, but not one of them could recall him ever mentioning the famous costume.[1] It is possible that it was never consciously designed at all, and that the instructions for making the costume, which probably appeared quite unremarkable at the time, may have been only roughly indicated on a scrap of paper which was discarded with the studio rubbish.

The main features of the Sylphide costume were its simple style and silhouette and its whiteness. Apart from the crown of flowers which Taglioni wore on her head and the peacock-feather wings attached to her shoulders, it differed little from the basic costume that a ballerina would have worn in class. Far from bursting on the world unheralded in *La Sylphide*, the Romantic tutu evolved gradually over a course of several years. Lecomte's cos-

tume for Montessu in *La Somnambule* (1827) already indicated the shape of things to come, and two years before *La Sylphide*, in the revival of *Flore et Zéphire*, Taglioni wore a costume of the same general design, differing only in the addition of floral decoration. In short, the Sylphide costume was remarkable not so much for any innovation of design as for its simplicity.

It is in the perspective of the historian that this costume has acquired its special significance. By complementing Taglioni's ethereal style of dancing it triggered a new image in the mind of the public, that of the Romantic ballerina, transmuted into a creature soaring amidst a mist of muslin, bound no longer by the physical laws of mankind. Its simple lines and full skirt emphasised the elegance of the figure, the dazzling whiteness of its material seemed a symbol of purity, while the layers of light white underskirts that floated around the moving body enhanced the illusion of weightlessness. All in all, it was the ideal costume for the dreamy moods of Romanticism, which were perhaps never more poetically conveyed than in the gas-lit forest scenes of *La Sylphide* and its successor in the same *genre*, *Giselle* (1841). It also played an essential part in the deification of the ballerina – at the expense, it must be noted, of the male dancer – that was such a noticeable feature of the Romantic ballet and a prime cause of the sterility into which ballet degenerated towards the end of the century.

It is interesting to trace the change in the shape of the Sylphide costume during the fifteen years Taglioni performed the role. A drawing by Laederich, made in 1832, shows the scene at the end of the ballet when the Sylphide kneels in despair at James's feet, her immortality destroyed by the bewitched scarf he has innocently placed on her shoulders. The skirt is only slightly bouffant, and the sleeves at her shoulders appear quite full. Another lithograph, by B. Mulrenin, dated 1834, shows the same characteristics, as does an 1840 lithograph by Lacauchie. But a few years later, in 1845, the glorious series of lithographs honouring Marie Taglioni, made from drawings by A.E. Chalon, and known as the 'Souvenir d'Adieu', reveals a significant change. Here the Romantic tutu is depicted in the fullness of its flowering, with the skirt spreading out, bell-shaped, from the tiny waist and – in spite of the increased number of underskirts – still giving an effect, through skilful use of material, of imponderable lightness. It was in a costume such as this that the great ballerina achieved her apotheosis in the celebrated *Pas de Quatre* of Perrot in 1845, a simple costume that, regarded dispassionately, was little more than an adaptation of a young girl's plain white ball dress of the period, with the skirt cut short below the knees.

The number of underskirts that had to be worn must have varied with individual taste and the fashion of the moment, but the wearing of drawers beneath the underskirts was obligatory. Generally these were white or flesh-coloured, but in Naples for a time they were green by Royal decree – passed after the Queen had been scandalised to see the gilded youth ogling the dancers through their opera glasses! A short, mildly erotic story by Ernest Feydeau, entitled *Le Cousu* and set at the Paris Opéra in 1843, included a specific description of the underwear that was worn at the Opéra at that time:

> Police regulations, which were very strict as regards the female personnel of the Opéra, required every danseuse appearing on the stage, whatever the costume, to wear beneath her short skirt, four underskirts of white gauze, one over the other, the first of which had to be stitched between the legs and was consequently known by the corps de ballet as the *cousu* to distinguish it from the others. This precaution, which is even imposed on the principal dancers, is taken to prevent accidents to the silk flesh-coloured drawers tied around their waists that might expose their most intimate charms to the curious gaze of the public.[2]

The ballet-girl of the 1840s in practice costume. *Bibliothèque Nationale*

In an age in which theatrical spectacle was becoming more and more appreciated by both critics and public, and when the *grand couturier* was beginning to be recognised as an artist in his own right, it is sadly ironic to find the costume designer still occupying a lowly status in the opera house. Théophile Gautier, for example, devoted much space in his reviews to describing the sets designed by Ciceri, Cambon, Thierry, Despléchin and other celebrated stage designers, but never once mentioned the designers of the costumes. To the outside world the costume designer was no more than an anonymous functionary working alongside the small work force of tailors and dressmakers. In fact, after Lecomte retired in 1831, the post of costume designer virtually lapsed and the task of designing devolved more and more on a young artist, Paul Lormier, who was subordinate to the head of the wardrobe department. Lormier thus had the distinction of devising the costumes for many of the important ballets produced at the Paris Opéra during the Romantic period, including *Giselle* (1841), but his designs were conventional and never particularly inspired. In 1855 he was promoted to the post of *chef d'habillement*, and with his administrative duties now taking up most of his time, he was content to pass the work of designing to an assistant, although he continued to produce occasional sketches for many years. Unhappily, this assistant, Alfred Albert, was also a man of unremarkable gifts, but so modest were the requirements for a costume designer that he retained his post for twenty years, producing designs that at best achieved a rather insipid prettiness, but offended no one and were no better and no worse than most of the ballet costumes designed for the other opera houses of Europe.

Nowhere had the possibilities of costume design been fully recognised. Opera house directors everywhere were content to entrust the designing of dancers' costumes to specialised employees on the regular payroll. Seldom was there a hard and fast distinction between the designing and making of costumes; sometimes the designer was expected to supervise the work of the tailors and dressmakers, sometimes those whose prime duty it was to make the costumes were also expected to design them, and costumes from earlier productions were often adapted for use again in a new work. Within these limitations, the costume designers, to whom the designation craftsman was often more apt than that of artist, nevertheless played an important part in the productions in which they were associated. In London, from the 1790s to 1821, the Superintendant of the Wardrobe, Signor Sestini, apparently had full responsibility for designing or selecting the costumes, but in the 1830s and 1840s, when the Romantic ballet attained its greatest popularity, no one was ever credited with designing the costumes, although the names of those who made them were sometimes recorded. In St. Petersburg the Imperial ballet had its regular costume makers who, unlike their Parisian

Marie Anne de Camargo by Lancret. *Wallace Collection*   Sylvie. *Boston Museum of Art*

Early experimenting on the points by an unidentified dancer. 1815. *Collection: Ivor Guest*

The anacreontic ballet in Romantic guise. Marie Taglioni in *Flore et Zéphire*. 1831. *Department of Prints and Drawings, V & A*

Inspiration from north-eastern Europe. *La Lituana* danced by Fanny Cerrito on her London debut, 1840. *Department of Prints and Drawings, V & A*

Costume design by Lucien Besche, probably for Pierina Legnani in Casati's ballet *Salandra*, 1890. *Department of Prints and Drawings, V & A*

The demure world
of the Paris Opéra
ballet in the 1870s
as seen by Degas.
*Glasgow Art
Gallery*

Costume design
by C. Wilhelm for
three butterflies in
Les Papillons, 1901.
*Department of
Prints and
Drawings, V & A*

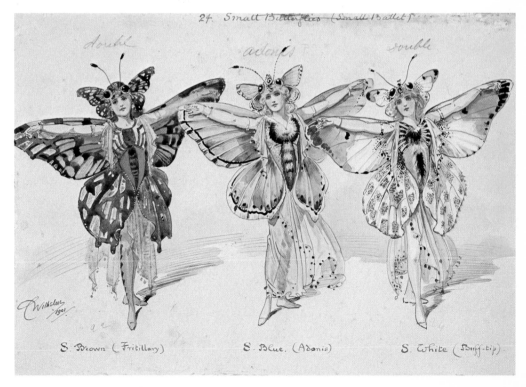

24. Small Butterflies (Small Ballet)

double · adonis · double

S. Brown (Fritillary) · S. Blue (Adonis) · S. White (Buff-tip)

The Etoile in her full
glory. Carlotta
Zambelli, 1897.
Musée de l'Opéra

counterparts, received credit for their work on the play-bills: Mathieu and Calvert, responsible for the men's costumes, and Mojarre and Stolyarov, who designed those for the women. And at the Scala, Milan, the costumes were commissioned from the same specialist costumiers season after season, notably Rossetti and Signora Majoli until 1824, Rovaglia from 1837 to 1851, and Zamperoni, who was associated with the Scala productions for more than forty years, from 1854 to 1896.

These designers were required to work in the conventional naturalistic manner of the time and were certainly not expected to exhibit any distinctive personal style. If, as was usual, a ballet had a plot set in a particular historical period or geographical setting, the characters who mimed the action or decorated the background – the Duke of Courland, Bathilde and the hunting party in *Giselle* (1841), for example – would be dressed in costumes that bore witness to the designer's familiarity with costume books but required no special effort of the imagination. The costumes of those with dancing roles, however, afforded greater scope for fantasy, and considerable ingenuity was displayed in suggesting character or nationality within the conventionally imposed limitations of style and silhouette.

Their legs clad in tights or knee breeches and stockings, male dancers were presented in costumes that ranged from the simple elegance of that which Lucien Petipa wore in the first act of *Giselle* (1841), through ornate costumes that in some cases could be very flattering and masculine, but in others gave an unfortunate impression of effeminacy, to the tasteless garb, more appropriate to a circus strong-man, that Louis Mérante had to wear in *L'Etoile de Messine* (1860). In conceiving costumes such as this last monstrosity, the designer no doubt subconsciously regarded the male dancer, whose role in ballet was being reduced to that of a mere *porteur* for the ballerina, as a glorified weight-lifter. At the other extreme, in centres where the male dancer was held in respect – in Paris in the days of Perrot and Lucien Petipa, in St. Petersburg when Johansson was in his prime, and most particularly in Copenhagen under Bournonville – the male dancer could be dressed to such advantage that his costume, in its unadorned simplicity, represents to this day the high-point of perfection of classical male dancing.

The costumes for the female dancers were kept rigidly within the standard silhouette of the Romantic tutu. Those for spirit creatures – sylphides, wilis, naiads, dryads, peris and others – followed the pattern set in *La Sylphide*, with or without wings, but tending, as the century progressed, to become over-decorated. The costume which Albert designed for Ferraris in *Les Elfes* (1856), for example, combined a full white Romantic tutu with a blue bodice rather heavily overlaid with imitation pearls, and a belt that seems somewhat inappropriate for the character. Another source of variety was the vogue for *couleur*

locale, a feature of Romantic art that was no less prominent than its obsession with the supernatural. The ballet-going public evinced an unquenchable interest in distant and exotic lands, which provided choreographers, in common with artists in other idioms, with a rich and seemingly inexhaustable source of material. Spain and Italy, Germany, Poland, Russia and the Middle East, India all inspired settings for successful ballets during the mid-nineteenth century, and it was the costume designer's task to reproduce the appropriate national costume, adapted as necessary to accommodate the steps of the choreography and, of course, to accord with European taste. This he did by retaining the basic silhouette of the Romantic tutu and suggesting national characteristics by the colour and decoration of bodice and skirt, and the addition perhaps of a bolero jacket, a head-dress or a veil, the hair-styling, or – where the style of the choreography permitted – the substitution of boots for conventional ballet shoes. In the interests of decency some details had to be excluded such as bare breasts, which for goddesses of antiquity were chastely suggested

The male dancer reduced to the statue of a strong man. Louis Mérante supporting Amalia Ferraris in *L'Etoile de Messine* at the Paris Opéra in 1860. *Bibliothèque Nationale*

LE MALAPOU,
OR
THE LOVE DANCE,
Performed by
THE BAYADERES,
Amany, Tille, Saundirounn, and Ramgoun,
at the
Theatre Royal Adelphi,
Composed by
J. J. MASSET.

Ent. Sta. Hall.

Price 2/-

by the design on the bodice, and rings in the nose such as Amani, the bayadere dancer from India, displayed when she danced in Paris and London in 1838.

The most celebrated national dance performed on the ballet stage in Romantic times was unquestionably the Cachucha, which created a furore when Fanny Elssler introduced it in the ballet *Le Diable boiteux* in Paris in 1836. What made it so distinctive was its authenticity, for it was constructed from genuine elements of the Spanish classical school, the *escuela bolera*, and performed to the traditional Cachucha melody. The costume which Elssler wore for it – made, no doubt, by the Opera's costumiers, but obviously modelled on the dresses which a group of Spanish dancers had worn when visiting Paris two years

earlier – was no less authentically Spanish in style and cut, being made from pink satin extensively trimmed and decorated with black lace, the skirt falling to a point midway between knee and ankle. This costume caught the imagination of the public hardly less forcefully than the Sylphide tutu, as representing the earthly, in distinction to the aerial, aspect of Romantic ballet. The Cachucha soon had its imitators, as other ballerinas exploited the vogue for things Spanish, but the costumes they wore reverted noticeably to the conventional shape of the ballet tutu, and perhaps their dances too were more 'balletic' in conception. But, on the other hand, Spanish dance companies were equally affected by the fashions of the time, and when Josefa Vargas, Petra Cámara and Perea Nena toured Europe in the 1840s and 1850s, the style of their costumes revealed the same influences that had been at work in the field of ballet.

The authentic Bayadères, Amani on the left with ring in her nose. *Collection: Ivor Guest (left)*

The Orient through the eyes of the ballet costumier. Marie Taglioni in *La Bayadère. Department of Prints and Drawings, V & A*

Spanish dance brought to the Romantic ballet stage. Fanny Elssler in her costume for the 'Cachucha', first danced by her at the Paris Opéra in *Le Diable boiteux*, 1836. *Collection: Ivor Guest*

The Cachucha was only the most famous of scores of national and pseudo-national dances that made their way into ballets at this time. Elssler herself followed it with a Cracovienne in *La Gipsy* (1839) and a tarantella in *La Tarantule* (1840); not to be outdone, Taglioni brought back a mazurka from Russia in 1838, and Cerrito danced a

The Romantic ballet silhouette adopted by Spanish dancers. Perea Nena. *Collection: Ivor Guest (left)*

The polka craze on the stage. Jules Perrot and Carlotta Grisi in the version they danced at Her Majesty's Theatre, London, in 1844. *Department of Prints and Drawings, V & A*

so-called Lithuanian number at her London debut in 1840, wearing a fetching fur-trimmed costume and boots. In 1844 the polka craze not only conquered the ballrooms but quickly invaded the theatres, with such variants as the Opera House Polka which Perrot and Carlotta Grisi danced in scarlet costumes of an unmistakably Polish character, and the Redowa Polka of Cerrito and Saint-Léon. By the 1850s few ballets were produced that did not include a *pas de caractère* of some sort, and this custom was still strong in 1870, when *Coppélia* was produced with its famous czardas, and no less in evidence more than twenty years later when Petipa produced the ballroom act

of *Swan Lake* (1895). The part played by the costume designers in satisfying the demand for national dances was an important one, and great skill was displayed in the creation of colourful costumes of seemingly infinite variety from the vast treasure-store of European folk art.

Lithographs, engravings and drawings abound showing dancers of this time in performance, but there is little record of how they appeared at class or at an ordinary rehearsal. Mrs. Grote's drawing of Fanny Elssler in practice costume is almost a unique record of what a ballerina wore around 1840 for the gruelling preparation she went through to acquire and maintain her technique, and the costumes of dancers of more modest status were not markedly different. In the School of Dance of the Paris Opéra the dancers changed into a practical costume which Albéric Second described in his amusing survey of life behind the scenes, *Les Petits Mystères de l'Opéra*, published in 1844:

> The girls are bare-headed, their shoulders and arms are uncovered, and their waists confined in a tight bodice. A very short, very bouffant skirt of net or striped muslin reaches to the knees. Their thighs are chastely concealed beneath large calico drawers that are as impregnable as a State Secret. The men are open-necked, and wear short jackets of white piqué and breeches half way down the leg, held at the waist by a leather belt. It is almost stage costume, but you are aware that there is a world of difference between 'almost' and 'exactly'. It is, in fact, stage costume without the illusion of lighting and the deceptive attraction of wet-white and vegetable rouge. I hasten to add that a dancer in class is not very captivating and not at all poetic. Her complexion is freckled, blotchy and spotted, her eyes are dull and lacklustre, her mouth unsmiling. She is out of breath, exhausted, worn out. She perspires dreadfully, the sweat staining her bodice and standing out in countless beads on her forehead and her arms.[3]

With rather less realistic detail, E. de Beaumont recorded glimpses of the Paris Opéra dancers in their practice costume in his series of caricatures, 'L'Opéra au XIXᵉ siècle', published in the satirical paper, *Le Charivari*, in 1844 and 1845.

For the humbler ranks of the corps de ballet matters were very different. Choreography was very much concentrated on the principals and the leading soloists, and ensemble dances, in which the corps de ballet participated, demanded no special display of skill. Jules Perrot's use of the corps de ballet for expressive crowd scenes in *La Esmeralda* (1844) was considered very innovatory, and when he produced a *pas de neuf* for nine principals and soloists in *Lalla Rookh* (1846), the critics remarked particularly upon the complexity of the choreography. The corps de ballet filled mainly a decorative role, and was not

required to take daily class, as were the leading ballerinas and aspiring soloists who toiled each morning to preserve and improve their technique. Albert Smith, in his *Natural History of the Ballet Girl* (London, 1847), depicted scenes in the life of a corps de ballet dancer in London at that time. Introducing a child attending a dancing lesson, he described her as wearing a knee-length ballet skirt, with her ordinary clothes above the waist. Young dancers of ambition had to work as hard then as they do today, but coming as they usually did from the poorer classes of society, few could have afforded a regular practice costume for class and no doubt many did no more than exchange their long skirt for a lighter, shorter one, as Smith's child did. Indeed Smith described a rehearsal of the corps de ballet in which the women wore their street clothes, merely having removed their bonnets and shawls, some having tied handkerchiefs, gypsy fashion, over their heads, and – a curious detail – all of them wearing gloves.

On the strength of Smith's description alone, it would no doubt be wrong to draw a general conclusion that the corps de ballet always attended rehearsals in their street clothes. It was certainly otherwise at the Paris Opéra, and Perrot was apparently accustomed to rehearsing the corps de ballet at Her Majesty's Theatre, London, in practice costume in the 1840s, for one of his first acts on arriving in St. Petersburg in 1848 was to impose this rule there. Surprised to find the Russian corps de ballet dancers waiting for him in everyday attire, he vigorously objected, only to be told by the regisseur that they were not required to take daily class and did not possess tutus. When he insisted, it was pointed out that they were paid very little. But Perrot persevered and eventually had his way with surprisingly little resistance from the dancers themselves, who, finding themselves rewarded with a more prominent part in his ballets, began to take a greater pride in their work.

With the increasing demands that ballet technique placed on the feet, shoes became a vitally important article of a dancer's equipment. This was particularly true of the female dancers, who were assimilating and exploiting the possibilities of *pointe* work. At the beginning of the century, they wore light satin slippers with flexible leather soles and ribbons for tying round the ankle. Even when *pointe* work began to be developed in the Romantic period, the style of shoe remained basically unchanged. There was no block at the toe, and the shoe differed little from the slippers that were worn in the ballroom. However, as *pointe* work grew more demanding, strengthening at the toe became necessary, but at first this was done by the dancers themselves by darning the tip and then inserting wadding to protect the toes.

By the 1860s manufacturers were producing shoes that were specifically designed to assist the dancer to accomplish the growing vocabulary of feats on *pointe*. The adaptation, however, was slight, as a comparison of the shoes worn by Taglioni in the 1830s and by Emma Livry in the early 1860s reveals, but a degree of reinforcement was already necessary. In an essay written in 1866, Théophile Gautier gave a carefully detailed description of the ballet slipper as it had developed up to that date:

> The sole, which is very hollowed out in the centre, does not reach the tip of the foot but ends squarely, leaving about two finger-breadths of material projecting. The purpose of this is to enable the dancer to perform *pointe* work by giving a sort of jointed point of support, but as the whole weight of the body is borne on this part of the shoes, which would inevitably

break, the dancer has to strengthen it by darning, very much as old-clothes menders do to the heels of stockings to make them last. The inside of the shoe is lined with strong canvas and, at the very end, a strip of leather and cardboard, the thickness of which depends on the lightness of the wearer. The rest of the shoe is chevronned on the outside by a network of ribbons firmly sewn on, and there is also stitching on the quarter, which is adjusted by a little tag of ribbon in the Andalusian manner.[4]

The manufacture of ballet shoes was now becoming a specialised industry. At the height of the Romantic period one of the most successful shoemakers in this line was Janssen of Paris, who numbered both Taglioni and Elssler among his customers. Another celebrated Parisian manufacturer was Crait, whose shoes Saint-Léon ordered specially from St. Petersburg for his *protégée*, Adèle Grantzow, in 1865. The firm of Crait, which still flourishes today, was founded in Lyon in 1823, moved to Paris in 1850, and was appointed official suppliers of ballet shoes to the Paris Opéra in 1879, a distinction it has

Guiseppina Bozzachi wearing the costume designed by Alfred Albert for the doll scene in the first production of *Coppélia* in 1870. *Bibliothèque Nationale (below)*

The Degas dancer as seen by the photographer, A. Liébert. The dancer is probably Mlle. E. Parent. *Collection: Ivor Guest*

held ever since. Paris did not, of course, enjoy a complete monopoly; among the leading manufacturers elsewhere were Ebermann of Berlin, whose shoes Adeline Genée found ideally soft and pliant, and Romeo Niccolini of Milan, whose customers included many Russian dancers who had been impressed by the shoes he made for the Italian virtuosos who were the rage of St. Petersburg in the last fifteen years of the century. By that time ballet shoes were already being made with a 'block' at the toe, although, as photographs show, the reinforcement was inconspicuous and the shoe remained comparatively light.

Another item of clothing which formed an indispensable item in the dancer's wardrobe, were tights, which legend had it were invented early in the nineteenth century by a costumier called Maillot, by whose name they have been known ever since in France. It was important to keep tights and shoes unsoiled before the performance, and to protect them dancers had, by the 1840s, adopted the precaution of wearing gaiters of drill or other

Alfred Albert's design for the costume of Dawn in the last act of *Coppélia* (1870). *Musée de l'Opéra*

material until the time came for them to prepare for their entrance.

Throughout the 1850s and 1860s, the period of the Second Empire, the costumes worn in ballet showed little development in style. For the women the silhouette changed hardly at all, the length of the skirt remaining constant at a point just below the knees and its form retaining its bell-like shape, although, in line with the development of the crinoline, being now made more bouffant by the addition of more underskirts. The costumes which Giuseppina Bozzacchi wore for the creation of *Coppélia* in 1870 were distinguishable in style from those of Ferraris in *L'Etoile de Messine* ten years before only in the greater accretion of accessories such as headdresses, necklaces and bracelets. During the 1870s, however, a subtle variation of the silhouette echoed the introduction of the bustle in ladies' fashions, the skirt becoming noticeably fuller at the back than in front.

Meanwhile ballet technique had been making spectacular progress, and the extraordinary virtuosity that Milan-trained ballerinas were displaying in the area of *pointe* work was already compelling the admiration and wonder of all Europe. The shortening of the ballet skirt to give a better view of their *tours de force* was an inevitable consequence. By the mid-1870s Italian ballerinas had adopted the fashion of wearing the skirt several inches above the knee, and lowered the neckline of the bodice to a provocative level. The ballerina thus acquired a new image, part mechanical marvel, part symbol of sexuality, and certainly far removed from the idealised wraith of virginal purity that Taglioni had personified forty years before.

This trend, which was accepted only reluctantly by the opera houses of Europe for their native corps de ballet, was to be stimulated by the introduction of ballet into the less refined surroundings of the music hall. The second half of the nineteenth century witnessed the development of the music hall from modest saloons, where the working class sought their simple pleasures, into vast entertainment palaces drawing their public from every stratum of society. One of the earliest was the Alhambra Palace of Varieties in Leicester Square, which provided ballet with a base in London at a time when it had been virtually excluded from the opera houses of Covent Garden and Her Majesty's. Here, and shortly afterwards at the Empire Theatre, ballet found fertile soil in which to flourish, and though it had to do so in the company of variety acts of every description – comics, singers, acrobats, illusionists, performing animals, cyclists and eventually the biograph – it always occupied the place of honour, closing the programme, and sometimes both halves of the programme, in a blaze of spectacle. Of course the public came to the music hall not to savour the refinements of art, but to be entertained and to admire the girls. Nevertheless, ballet acquired a vitality there that was lacking in the opera house, and if the artistic impulse was weak, these popular theatres not only provided employment for a large number of dancers, including many leading ballerinas who had no reservations about appearing there, but during the forty years before the outbreak of World War I created a vast, if unsophisticated, new public for ballet. A high proportion of those who admired and supported the Diaghilev ballet in its early London seasons must have been weaned on the ballets at the Alhambra and the Empire.

The costume designers who worked at these music halls enjoyed a recognition never accorded to their predecessors in Romantic times. They also enjoyed considerably greater freedom. For one thing, the ballets presented at the music hall were much more varied in content than the conventional productions of the opera houses. Some indeed, such as Léon Espinosa's version of *The Sleeping Beauty* (1890), came from traditional moulds, but the divertissements revealed an astonishing diversity of ideas that stretched the ingenuity of the costumier to new limits. There were ballets about butterflies, birds and fish, Spanish, Barbaric, Turkish, Japanese ballets, carnival ballets, amazon ballets, military ballets, and no end of other varieties. At the end of the century a new type of ballet was making its appearance, the 'up to date ballet', which was based on a topical subject and was therefore costumed, not in the conventional styles prevailing in the opera house – except of course, for the ballerina when she came on to dance her variations – but in modern dress. Ballets of this sort had an instant appeal to the music hall audience, and were the forerunners of the ballet scenes that became a feature of revues and the inserted ballets in musical shows. Examples of such ballets in the 1890s were *Round the Town* (1892), which introduced such well-known London characters as Covent Garden market porters and the Salvation Army, *The Press* (1898), in which the dancers were dressed to represent contemporary newspapers and magazines, *Alaska* (1898), inspired by the Klondyke gold rush, and productions celebrating such occasions as Queen Victoria's Diamond Jubilee.

At the Alhambra the ballet costumes were for many years the responsibility of Charles Alias, an independent costumier who was to be equally renowned for his costumes for Christmas pantomimes. His association with the Alhambra began in the 1880s, when he was making the costumes from the designs of Lucien Besché, and later he worked from sketches by Howell Russell and Commelli. By the early 1890s he was being brought into the planning conferences along with the choreographer, composer, scenic artist, stage carpenter and machinist, and once the general scheme of the work had been decided upon, he would return to his studio in Soho Square to produce the costumes required. His encyclopaedic knowledge of his subject and his fanciful imagination earned him considerable respect, and on first

nights at the Alhambra he was given the privilege of taking a curtain call alongside the choreographer and the composer. This conscientious, hard-working man served the Alhambra ballet until it was disbanded in 1912, but he carried on his business until his death in 1921, when it was taken over by Nathan's.

From the artistic viewpoint the costumes for the ballets at the Empire attained a much greater distinction in that they were consciously conceived as part of the overall scenic design. This was due to one man, C. Wilhelm, who impressed his taste on costume design more potently than any other English artist of his time in the decades before the advent of the Diaghilev ballet. To all intents and purposes Wilhelm was the artistic director of the Empire ballet from the 1890s until it ceased to exist during the First World War. His real name was William John Charles Pitcher, and he was a ship-builder's son, born in Northfleet, Kent, in 1858. Theatrical spectacle had irresistibly fascinated him from the time he was a schoolboy, when he would return from his visits to the theatre able to reproduce from memory the settings he had seen. A natural, self-taught draughtsman, he developed a very personal style based on his own preferences, one of the strongest influences being the work of Gustave Doré. Apparently his parents were far from enthusiastic when he expressed the wish to follow a career in the theatre, for when he had his way he discreetly concealed his origins – for 'family reasons', as he put it – by adopting the professional name of Wilhelm. He was fortunate in being able to cultivate a number of useful contacts, and when he was still only nineteen, some of his sketches were accepted by the management of Drury Lane. A year later, in 1878, he was commissioned to design costumes for a ballet at the Alhambra called *The Golden Wreath*, and over the next six years he collaborated in three more ballets there before embarking on his life-long association with the Empire Theatre.

He designed the costumes for the Empire's inaugural production of Hervé's operetta, *Chilpéric*, in 1884, and three years later began to design regularly for the ballets that became the prominent feature of the programmes. Almost at once he made his presence felt as a man whose capabilities and ambition extended far beyond the limited confines of costume design, and before long he was undertaking wider responsibilities of artistic direction. His far-reaching responsibilities at the Empire presaged the contribution of Diaghilev's designers and placed him in a very different category from that of the opera house costume designer. He came to exercise a control over the whole scenic effect of a ballet and in some cases to be its principal creator, both writing the scenario and supervising the entire production. Undoubtedly the Empire ballet's remarkable stability and continuity owed much more to Wilhelm than to either of his two main colleagues, the choreographer Katti Lanner and the musical director

Léopold Wenzel, for his experience and flair in the field of ballet design in the widest sense was then quite unique.

The keynote of Wilhelm's method was a basic colour theme on which he would elaborate contrasts and harmonies to achieve a surprising variety of effects. In one production, for example, by the skilful injection of silver and gold and the use of different materials, he gave the impression that he had employed twenty different shades of blue when in fact he had used only four. He was particularly adept at producing brilliant climaxes, such as the splash of colours in the gigantic human bouquet that closed *Rose d'Amour* (1888), the jewels divertissement in *Monte Cristo* (1896), and the 'Roses of England' scene in *Our Crown* (1902). The impression created by such scenes as these, in which large numbers of dancers took part, redounded more to the credit of the designer than to that of the choreographer, for the technical means of the Empire corps de ballet were modest. Nor was Wilhelm afraid of experimenting with novel effects, such as the electric lights which the corps de ballet wore in their hair in *Diona* (1888). All this remarkable professional skill was combined with a scholar's attention to detail that was evident not only in his concern that his costumes should be perfectly executed, but also in an insistence on historical authenticity. At times, however, his preoccupation for detail was carried to excessive lengths, even by the opulent standards of Edwardian taste, as in his fastidious attempt to present the corps de ballet as recognisable varieties of lepidoptera in *Les Papillons* (1901).

Although he worked with equal ease in ballets on modern and historical themes, Wilhelm was at heart a conventional man and was never happier than when faced with reproducing a period scene. Among his most successful works in this genre were a series of dramatic ballets of his own devising which were presented at the Empire Theatre in the 1890s – *Orfeo* (1891), a treatment of the ancient Greek myth, *Versailles* (1892), in which he evoked the splendours of the court of Louis XIV, and *Faust* (1895).

The latter part of Wilhelm's career was closely linked to that of Adeline Genée, the Danish ballerina who made her debut at the Empire in 1897 and became one of the most prominent personalities of the Edwardian stage. Wilhelm designed the costumes for all the ballets in which she danced at the Empire. Of these, one of the most memorable was *Old China* (1901), with its delicately designed pageant of porcelain for which he demanded a pink stage cloth to complete the scenic illusion. The designer and the dancer, both perfectionists, became firm friends, and when Genée left the Empire and organised her own company, it was Wilhelm to whom she turned to design the costumes for her ballets. His designs for the period costumes in *La Camargo* and her historical survey of dancing, *La Danse* (both 1912), were conceived with a scholarly fidelity which Genée matched in her choreography and performance. Wilhelm retained his vigorous

imagination and love of colour to the end of his life, and one of his last creations for the theatre was a stunning dress in the modern style, with brightly-coloured panels, which Genée wore with delicious panache in *The Pretty Prentice* in the dark year of the Battle of the Somme, 1916.

At the end of his career Wilhelm had the misfortune to be submerged by a revolutionary change of taste, provoked by the powerful Slav exoticism of the Diaghilev ballet, which made his designs at once appear old-fashioned and fastidious. By then the world was already changing, and soon the age in which he had long been an arbiter of taste disintegrated in the fury of war and the frenzied search for pleasure of the 1920s. When he died in 1925 his contribution to the theatre had receded into history.

During the last quarter of the nineteenth century all vitality seemed to have gone out of the ballet at the Paris Opéra, where it had sunk to a sadly inferior level in comparison with the opera. While the ballet company remained numerically strong and the school continued its daily routine, ballet performances and new ballet productions became noticeably fewer. To thoughtful observers it must have been obvious that ballet had lost touch with the ideas that gave life to other artistic endeavours, for it was following formulae that had long since lost their relevance, and such appeal as it still possessed was stimulated largely by the glamour and technical exploits of a succession of Italian-trained ballerinas who headed the company – Sangalli, Mauri, Zambelli. It even lost touch with its own tradition; by 1890 the oldest ballet still being performed was *Coppélia* (1870), while *Giselle* had been dropped from the repertory since 1868.

In the costume department so little change could be perceived, either in the methods of working or in the style and quality of design, that the only distinguishing features of the designers seemed to be their names. In 1876 Alfred Albert was succeeded by Eugène Lacoste, who had studied under the celebrated stage designer Cambon, and who designed the costumes for *Sylvia* (1876), the first ballet to be created at the new opera house. In 1884 Lacoste was replaced in his turn by Charles Bianchini, who had served his apprenticeship by designing for revues and was to work for the Opéra until 1905, including among the ballets for which he designed *Namouna* (1882) and *Les Deux Pigeons* (1886). Bianchini also designed costumes for the Théâtre de Monte Carlo, some of which have survived to this day in that theatre's vast store.

The microcosm of the Paris Opéra ballet towards the close of the nineteenth century is today familiar from the sketches and paintings of Degas, which reveal very clearly how inward-looking it was. After making allowances for developments in the painter's style, the dancer of 1905 is hardly distinguishable from her predecessor of 1875. In fact, as photographs reveal, the regulation costume for class was not so flattering as Degas made it appear. The thighs were concealed, in class and at rehearsal, by ugly white drawers held in place just above the knees, and to the incorruptible camera lens the material was much less attractive than it appeared to the artist's eye.

Such developments in dancers' attire as took place in Paris during these years were to be found on stages outside the Opéra. The more commercially orientated popular theatres were always ready to present their dancers in titillating costumes, and as early as 1872 those for the insect ballet in Offenbach's *Le Roi Carotte* at the Théâtre de la Gaïté must have been as sexily suggestive as the law allowed. But there was another influence at

The sexy side of French ballet, as seen in the popular theatres in Paris in the 1870s. Mlle. Buisseret in the Insect Ballet in Offenbach's *Le Roi Carotte* at the Gaité. *Collection: Ivor Guest*

(below)

The ballerina reveals her charms in the shortened skirts of the 1880s, supported by her porteur. *Biblioteca Braidense, Milan*

work – the Italian fashion for shorter skirts, which burst upon Paris when the Eden-Théâtre opened in 1883. This was a vast entertainment palace – in conception, akin to the great plush music halls in London's Leicester Square – which was inaugurated with a mixed bill of circus and Italian ballet. The opening ballet was Manzotti's *Excelsior*, whose theme was not a fantasy about ethereal spirits but a review of the progress of the modern world. The technical marvels performed by the ballerina Elena Cornalba, the metronomical precision of the corps de ballet, and the abbreviated costumes of the ballerinas made a vivid impression on the Parisian public, and the ballet ran nightly for many months. In the next ballet production, Manzotti's *Sieba*, Cornalba was joined by another prima ballerina, Virginia Zucchi, whose valkyrie costume revealed the curves of her figure to a degree that would never have been tolerated at the Opéra.

The Eden itself was short-lived, but the extraordinary technique of the Italian ballerinas created a lasting impression. It was in this area of purely physical accomplishment that the most striking developments in ballet were

taking place in the latter part of the nineteenth century. For many years the ballet schools of Milan had been turning out virtuosos who seemed to be continually inventing new tours de force, almost as if they were acrobats rather than dancers, and concentrating the public's attention on the legs and feet. In the 1840s and 1850s Sofia Fuoco, Caterina Beretta and Amalia Ferraris had given Paris a foretaste of what was to come, and now, thirty years later, Italian ballerinas held a virtual monopoly of the star positions throughout Europe: in Paris, Sangalli and Mauri (who was Italian-trained, though Spanish by birth); Zucchi (who was, however, more a dramatic dancer than a virtuoso), Maria Giuri, Sozo and Limido paving the way in the summer theatres of St. Petersburg; Dell'Era in Berlin, and Cerale and Pagliero in Vienna.

More than ever before the ballerina was the centre of attraction, her appearance awaited with such eager anticipation that the rest of the ballet receded into insignificance. Her ascendancy was affirmed both by her virtuosity and by her costume. An English visitor to Bologna in 1883, chancing to see a performance of *Excelsior* with Maria Giuri, was treated to a dazzling demonstration of the magic with which a ballerina could bewitch her public:

> Then the *prima ballerina assoluta*, Maria Giuri, a fair young girl of seventeen, from Trieste, appeared in the midst of the corps de ballet, dressed in white gauze, with the short skirts worn in Italy, and danced a 'variation' alone. At times her feet seemed hardly to touch the ground, for she danced on her extreme points, and appeared to fly through the air like a feather, performing the most fantastical and difficult steps, while her pirouettes and *ronds de jambe* excited the utmost enthusiasm, as she constantly made from thirty to thirty-five without resting on the other foot.[5]

Clearly this is a reference to those multiple *ronds de jambe fouettés en dehors* that represented the very summit of virtuosity and are today preserved in the Black Swan *pas de deux* in *Swan Lake*. Although it has come to be associated particularly with Pierina Legnani, this feat appears to have been included in the technical vocabulary of most Italian ballerinas around 1890. Legnani is recorded as having performed a sequence of thirty-two in London in 1893, before going to St. Petersburg. The above description, however, establishes a prior claim for Maria Giuri, for it can be dated ten years earlier, to the autumn of 1883, when she was dancing in *Excelsior* at the Teatro Comunale in Bologna. Carlotta Zambelli, who knew both Legnani and Giuri, told the writer that Giuri was performing multiple *fouettés* at the Scala, Milan, when she, Zambelli, was a pupil there (1888–93). And it takes no great stretch of the imagination to realise how essential was the shortened tutu, which would develop

into the now familiar platelike form during the twentieth century, if the execution of such feats was to be fully appreciated.

Belatedly even the Paris Opéra had to take note of the Italian skirt length, and by 1890 its leading dancers were proudly standing before the camera in skirts cut several inches above the knee. Strangely enough, though, Carlotta Zambelli, although born and trained in Milan, abjured this fashion, favouring the traditional knee-length ballet skirts.

In St. Petersburg the Italian length had been introduced at the Imperial Theatres some years earlier, in 1885, when Virginia Zucchi was first engaged. At the first sight of the costume she was expected to wear in Marius Petipa's *Daughter of Pharaoh*, she was so appalled at the old-fashioned length that, in flagrant defiance of the regulations, she took a pair of scissors and cut the skirt to her own taste, saying she refused to dance in a costume fit only for her grandmother. She had her way, and her example was followed by the other Italian ballerinas who succeeded her in St. Petersburg, as well as by native-born Russian dancers.

At the Imperial Theatres in Russia the designing of ballet costumes was entrusted to specialist artists on the staff in the same way as at the Paris Opéra. There was little attempt to achieve artistic unity in the general conception of a production, each artist being left to work independently of the others. As in Paris, too, the task of producing the scenery was often apportioned between several scenic artists, each of whom had his own speciality – interiors, landscapes or sea scenes, for example – while the costumes and properties fell within the domain of other departments. Usually it was not until the dress rehearsal that the overall result could be fully judged for the first time. The choice of a single artist to design a complete ballet production, such as was happening in a modest way under Wilhelm at the Empire Theatre and would be the great innovation of the Diaghilev ballet, was still an unheard of procedure in St. Petersburg when the century closed.

There was, however, a significant degree of artistic coordination being exercised at the Maryinsky Theatre towards the end of the century by Ivan Vsevolozhsky, who directed the Imperial Theatres in St. Petersburg from 1881 to 1899. Vsevolozhsky saw ballet as an important element in the artistic activity committed to his charge, and did much to improve its quality and enhance its appeal by exploiting the vogue for Italian virtuosos and, more significantly, by reawakening Tchaikowsky's interest in the ballet and enriching the repertory with *The Sleeping Beauty* (1890), *The Nutcracker* (1892) and *Swan Lake*

Nineteenth century ballet costume at its most revealing. Virginia Zucchi's valkyrie costume in Manzotti's ballet *Sieba*. *Harvard Theatre Collection*

(1895). The first of these created a profound impression not merely by its rich, melodious score and the choreography by the seemingly immortal Marius Petipa, but by the freshness and splendour of the production as a whole. Alexandre Benois, who was to be one of the greatest ballet designers of the next century, was dazzled by it when he first saw it as a young man of twenty, and in his memoirs recognised it as a landmark in that it had revived traditions of the St. Petersburg ballet that had become smothered by routine:

Design by Evgeny Ponomarev for Odette's costume in Act II of the St. Petersburg production of *Swan Lake* (1895). *Collection: Ivor Guest (below)*

Ponomarev's costume as worn by Pierina Legnani in *Swan Lake* (1895). *Museo alla Scala, Milan*

Chief credit for this belongs to Vsevolozhsky . . . He was the person responsible for *creating this masterpiece*, for he made the production of the ballet his own personal work. It was he who, by entering into all the details, became the link as well as the head of the whole production – a feature indispensable in the creation of a *Gesamtkunstwerk*. This resulted in a coherence and polish hitherto unseen.[6]

In his endeavours to achieve artistic cohesion, Vsevolozhsky was treading the same path as Wilhelm, but the parallel between the two men can be carried further, for both chose to exercise their talent specifically in the field of costume design. During his eighteen years as director, Vsevolozhsky designed the costumes for a number of important productions, the most celebrated of which was *The Sleeping Beauty*. He was fully professional

Practice costume at the Paris Opéra at the turn of the century. Carlotta Zambelli, Mlle. Boos, Mlle. Vangoethem, Clotilde Piodi. *'Le Théâtre'* Dec. 1898

in the manner in which he performed his chosen duties, producing a complete set of sketches (one hundred and twenty in all), each one a finished study, adding technical directions for the costumiers, selecting the fabrics to be used, and supervising the making of the costumes at every stage. If his designs could be criticised, as they were by Benois, for their 'rather helpless amateurishness,' they blended well enough with the conventional scenery of the period and contributed positively towards the overall effect. However, they were not remarkable for any particular individuality, nor did they reveal any trace of the barbaric strength of the nationalist trend that was making itself felt in Russian art outside establishment circles. Vsevolozhsky's taste was, in fact, that of a courtier, which was, of course, what he was. A reflection of the hothouse atmosphere of the court and St. Petersburg society, it was consciously influenced by French models. *The Sleeping Beauty* was essentially an expression of

French culture, being based on a French fairy tale and dressed in costumes that evoked two specific periods of the French monarchy, the colourful mid-sixteenth century for the first part and, after the awakening, the pomp and panache of the early years of the Sun King's reign.

Nor was there anything particularly Russian in the other ballets for which he designed. *The Nutcracker* had a German flavour in its opening scene of the children's party, while Clara's dream, with its culminating divertissement in the Kingdom of Sweets, was the sort of fantasy that (if one overlooks the infinitely superior dancing of the Russians) would not have been out of place at the Alhambra or the Empire. Another of his important productions, *Raymonda* (1898), was set in Provence, with the injection of exotic colour in the form of some striking Hungarian and Saracen costumes, while his last work for the Maryinsky, *Ruses d'Amour* (1900), could hardly have been more French in its inspiration, being based directly on the drawings of Watteau.

Prudently, Vsevolozhsky kept his involvement as costume designer anonymous, but once he had ceased to be Director, he allowed the secret to be revealed in an article

The subservience of the male dancer. Miguel Vasquez flanked by Mlles. Lobstein and Viollat. *'Le Théâtre'* Dec. 1898

by Evgeny Ponomarev in the *Yearbook of the Imperial Theatres* for 1899–1900. Ponomarev had been engaged as artist and librarian in 1887, and worked as Vsevolozhsky's principal lieutenant in the costume department, assisting his master by undertaking the research needed to achieve the authenticity that seemed to be prized even above artistic quality, and being ready to design costumes when the Director was not disposed to do so himself. In this way Ponomarev found himself entrusted with the task of collaborating in the Petipa/Ivanov production of *Swan Lake*. He was an industrious man of very ordinary gifts who was in no danger of outshining Vsevolozhsky, and who produced costumes that a contemporary described as 'conventional, almost to the point of uniformity.'[7]

As yet there was no serious movement towards reforming the scenic department at the Maryinsky, for things had been managed thus since time immemorial, and in an ultra-conservative organisation like the Imperial Theatres it would have been almost treasonable to question procedures that were hallowed by tradition. But as the new century dawned, a generation was emerging that was to

rethink the principles of theatrical art for itself. While Stanislavsky, Craig and Appia were bringing their minds to bear on the wider issues of theatrical production, young painters like Benois and Bakst were realising that stage design offered exciting opportunities to the major artist and should no longer be a branch of art reserved for the specialised artist-craftsman. And there was questioning even within the company itself, by intelligent young dancers who were becoming aware of the weaknesses in the apparatus of the Imperial ballet – the poverty of ideas in the conception of a ballet, the lack of artistic cohesion in production, and the obsessive concentration on the technical brilliance of the prima ballerina, whose regulation tutu never varied in silhouette, suggesting the period or setting of the action only by the colour and decoration of the material, with perhaps some minor accessory such as an apron or quiver of arrows.

These weaknesses were universal, but it was in Russia that the much-needed reform was to originate. Petipa was to retire, at last, in 1903, leaving the way clear for Mikhail Fokine to emerge as the first great choreographer of the new century; and in less than a decade the Diaghilev ballet was launched on its meteoric mission to establish ballet as a major performing art. In the process many of the absurdities of the past were to be swept away, but underneath there remained the solid foundations that had been laid in earlier times by countless men and women who had dutifully performed their various tasks. And among them, occupying a significant and honourable place, were those who designed and made the costumes, their contribution forming as essential a part of the balletic heritage as the performances of those who wore them.

References

1. Carlos Fischer, *Les Costumes de l'Opéra* (Paris 1931), pp.208–211.
2. Ernest Feydeau, *Le Cousu* (Paris, 1872), p.11.
3. Albéric Second, *Les Petits Mystères de l'Opéra* (Paris, 1844), pp.180–181.
4. Théophile Gautier, *Le Peau de tigre* (Paris 1866), pp.335–336.
5. Anon, *More Society Recollections* (London, n.d.), p.264.
6. Alexandre Benois, *Reminiscences of the Russian Ballet* (London, 1941), p.131.
7. Prince Peter Lieven, *The Birth of the Ballets-Russes* (London, 1936), p.67.

Modern Ballet
Design: 1909–1980

RICHARD BUCKLE

The diminishing role of the designer

Is the designer really necessary? Today, the better the ballet the less need there is for a costume. I don't mean that dancers should let it all hang out; for total nudity, of which the Dutch and Danish Ballets have given us glimpses on the stage, is unbecoming to bodies in motion. Isadora Duncan's flimsy breast-revealing Greek chiton may have influenced women to abandon the corset in everyday life: few dancers have wished to follow her example. Balletic nudity must be stylized like balletic copulation. What the French call *'un maillot collant'*, what the Americans call the 'body stocking', and what I call 'all-over tights' is the equivalent of nudity on the ballet stage. Nor do the additions of a silk tunic, a wisp of drapery or a vestigial skirt to make a woman more feminine detract from this, any more than in the nineteenth century the short *tutu* destroyed the noble geometry of Petipa.

No good sculptor would want to sculpt a man in top hat, white tie and tails (except, as Nadelman did, for purposes of social satire) if he could sculpt him nude. In the same way the good choreographer, a sculptor of bodies in motion, will resent the concealment of his lines and loops and tangles by a lot of trimmings. In the early 1930s, when ballet was taking root in England and America, there were naturally few well trained dancers – particularly male dancers – and ballets tended to be eked out with drama and decoration in order to camouflage this deficiency. Today, dancing has grown more technically perfect, there are innumerable excellent dancers, and Balanchine has made the best ballets in history. Most of these, such as Stravinsky's *Agon* or his *Symphony in Three Movements* have been dressed in tights and T-shirts, which are thrown away when they shrink or wear out. They will not therefore be found in this exhibition, any more than the costumes for *Monotones*, perhaps Ashton's finest ballet.

In November 1947 André Derain came to London to stage *Mam'zelle Angot* for the Royal Ballet; and I remember Ninette de Valois repeating to me a remark he made to her: 'You can't invent a theatrical costume. You find it all in old books.' Now, Derain was a painter with a real feeling for the theatre. What he meant was that when you make a ballet with a national character, or one set in an historical period, you must do your homework and absorb the correct style before allowing your fantasy to take over. Before designing *La Boutique fantasque* for Massine and Diaghilev (1919), *L'Epreuve d'Amour* for Fokine

and René Blum's Ballets de Monte Carlo (1936), and *Mam'zelle Angot* for Massine and the Royal Ballet (then called Sadler's Wells) (1947), he had looked up respectively fashion plates of the 1870s, eighteenth-century *chinoiseries* and prints of the *Directoire*. His simplifications of the period styles, conceived with an infallible sense of colour and set against landscapes or streetscapes in which he gave a freer rein to his personal manner of painting, were wonderfully successful. But Derain, to my knowledge, had never been asked to design a classical – as opposed to a character or *demi-caractère* – ballet.

The evolution of modern ballet has been from the character to the classical. By 'modern ballet' I mean ballet between May 1909, when Diaghilev's Russian troupe appeared in Paris, and the present day. Diaghilev's revelation, though it was one of music, design and dancing as well as of choreography, was based on Fokine's revolution against the standard form of nineteenth-century ballet in Russia. Because Fokine wanted to be totally free from the old conventions of silk tights, tarlatan *tutus* and blocked satin slippers (just as he determined to abolish the set-piece solos and *pas de deux* and the symmetry of the *corps de ballet*), the new costumes for his music dramas designed by Benois, Bakst and Roerich were convincing Russian, Persian, Indian or ancient Greek creations, as 'realistic' as the brushes of these new designers – whom the French called 'impressionistic' – would allow. With rare exceptions – *Le Pavillon d'Armide*, *Les Sylphides*, *Carnaval* (all three period *pastiches*) and *Le Spectre de la rose* – Diaghilev's new works were character ballets. I had cause to observe, when writing the lives of Nijinsky and Diaghilev, that by 1912 'the only female dancer – with two exceptions – who was called upon to stand *sur les pointes* during the Paris season was Karsavina in *Le Spectre*, *L'Oiseau de feu* and *Petrushka*. The two exceptions were the two street dancers in the last ballet.'

When Nijinsky and Stravinsky made *The Rite of Spring* in 1913 both music and choreography were incredibly new and daring, but Roerich's baggy Russian peasant costumes, many of which are in the collection of our Theatre Museum, were realistic in the sense that they were what he imagined Russian peasants actually wore in prehistoric times. So *The Rite* marked no advance in design.

When Massine succeeded Fokine and Nijinsky as Diaghilev's choreographer his first creation was a Russian character ballet, *Soleil de Nuit* (1916); and the nature of his *demi-caractère* ballets which followed was conditioned as much by his own limited classical technique

GOING GREEK. Isadora Duncan. Isadora dancing to Gluck.
Drawing by José Clara.

and by the shortage of good classically trained dancers
available from Russia as by the desire, born from the
Ballet's wartime wanderings in Italy and Spain, to invent
comedies of manners with an Italian or Spanish accent.
Massine made no classical ballets at that time. Although
for the lavish pre-war exoticism of Russian painters, he
substituted a new simplicity of design which was in keep-
ing with the thinner orchestration of the mature
Stravinsky and of the young French composers, Massine
was still producing ballets in which the sculpture of
bodies was less emphasised and less striking than characterization and expression.

In 1921, when Diaghilev found himself without a
choreographer, he staged the old evening-long masterpiece of Tchaikovsky and Petipa, *The Sleeping Beauty*, in
London. This could be regarded as a step backwards and
a denial of all his innovations (and that is how the intellec-
tuals of Bloomsbury saw it): but this extravagant production, which nearly ruined Diaghilev, not only provided
an opportunity for Bakst to give a virtuoso display of
eighteenth-century *pastiche*, but heralded a return to
classicism. The classical tradition is impossible to sustain
without sound schooling; and many dancers who took

GOING GREEK. Leon Bakst. Design for Lykenion in *Daphnis et
Chloë*. Department of Prints & Drawings, V & A

part in this 'disastrous' enterprise lived to hand on the
precepts of Petipa to students in England, Europe and
America.

The Sleeping Beauty, which Diaghilev chose to call *The
Sleeping Princess*, can be seen now as a portent. A year
later Bronislava Nijinska in *Les Noces* (1923) even made
her Russian peasant girls (clad in a monochrome uniform
by Nathalie Gontcharova) dance on point. Her *chic* neo-

GOING GREEK. Albert Rutherston. Design for Flora (Pavlova) in *Le Réveil de Flore. Department of Prints & Drawings, V & A*

GOING GREEK. Juan Gris. Design for Daphnis (Dolin) in *Daphnis et Chloë* (1924 revival). *Theatre Museum, V & A*

classical dances in the drawing-room comedy of *Les Biches*, for which Marie Laurencin designed a cross between classical ballet costume and modern dress, could be said to have prepared the ground in January 1924 for the work of Balanchine, who arrived from Soviet Russia later in the year. It was Balanchine, the heir of Petipa, who not only gave a new direction to the dance itself, but because of the nature of his choreography decided the new trend in dance costume. In 1928 (the year in which *Apollon Musagète*, now called *Apollo*, paired Balanchine with Stravinsky for the first time) another Russian exile, Pavel Tchelishchev, whose name is always simplified to Tchelitchev, designed for Massine's *Ode* the first white unadorned all-over tights or body stockings ever worn on the ballet stage. For women this was even more drastic than for men, and Doubrovska felt like Eve after she had bitten the apple. (In fact, the fifteen-year-old Maskova had worn such a white *maillot* in *Le Chant du Rossignol* in 1925, but this had been in the nature of a special improvisation by Matisse, Balanchine and Diaghilev, as Kassarina's former costume, adorned with veils and white roses, looked too fussy on her undeveloped figure.) As a designer Tchelitchev's influence would be almost as potent as that of Balanchine in choreography and Stravinsky in music. All three of these men would extend the frontiers of their art in the United States, where Lincoln Kirstein invited Balanchine in 1933, where Tchelitchev moved in 1935, and where Stravinsky took up residence in 1940. Of the three, perhaps only Tchelitchev, the most prophetic (in the way that poets sometimes are, but rarely painters), foresaw the New Age in ballet, when lighting would replace paint, when dancers would be stripped to the quasi-nudity of classical or

ROMANTIC BALLET. Cecil Beaton. Design for the Woman in Balldress (Fonteyn) in *Apparitions. Royal Ballet Benevolent Fund*

renaissance statues, when Balanchine would spread a new universal language of the dance – a kind of Russo-American Esperanto – and when this choreographer's many-sided genius would seem to diminish the stage designer's importance, and go far towards abolishing him altogether.

It is hard in an exhibition to illustrate as clearly as one would like a trend or tendency such as I have indicated, for the costumes for certain crucial ballets may not be available, or may have ceased to exist. All one can show are examples of the various tasks a designer may be called upon to undertake, and the wide variety of artists who have produced designs for ballet costume. Some of the most handsome costumes may be by designers who have swum against the current of the age.

As Derain had realized, much of the work demanded of a designer is a matter of *pastiche*. He may be asked to evoke Spain, ancient Greece, the Orient, the eighteenth

ROMANTIC BALLET. Christian Bérard. Design for the Beloved (Toumanova) in *Symphonie Fantastique. Theatre Museum, V & A*

ROMANTIC BALLET. Jean Hugo. Design for the Poet's Muse (Fonteyn) in *circa 1830. Collection of the Artist*

century, the Romantic period, the Wild West. I have tried in a small way to show in the illustrations to this chapter how different designers have tackled similar problems. The reader will find comparisons of 'Ancient Greek', eighteenth-century and 'Romantic' costumes designed during the last seventy years.

To adapt modern dress to the exigencies of ballet is almost a branch of *pastiche*. Several interesting designers have done this very successfully. As everyday clothes became simpler, so it became easier for the designer and choreographer to make the classic dance relate to real life.

When is a stage designer not a stage designer? When he is an 'easel painter'. This is an awkward if accepted expression for an artist who works as a painter pure and simple; and in our context it means a painter whose reputation is independent of his stage designs. Most of Diaghilev's designers were easel painters, and some were even sculptors. He had an instinct for turning men of talent or genius to the service of his theatre, just as he knew how to extract ballet scores from composers who

would otherwise have scorned to write ballet music. Since Diaghilev's day fewer outstanding artists have been lured to work for ballet; and those who have done so have not always met with success.

The Diaghilev Period, 1909–1929

Diaghilev's first designers were St. Petersburg painters whose work he had exhibited or who had illustrated his magazine *The World of Art* (1899–1904). Benois was in love with old St. Petersburg, with Versailles and the eighteenth century, and with the Romantic period. He was the subtlest of *pasticheurs*. His *Pavillon d'Armide* (1909) gave an individual and fantastic twist to the splendours of Louis XIV; his *Sylphides* (1909) evoked the reveries of Chopin; his *Petrushka* (1911) brought the St. Petersburg of 1830 to life. Roerich was in love with prehistoric or primitive Russia. He provided the designs for *Prince Igor* and *The Rite of Spring* which enhanced Borodin's inebriating music for the former, though they hardly paralleled the novelty of Stravinsky's score for the latter. Bakst, though capable of adapting himself to Romantic ideas, as in *Carnaval* (1910) and *Le Spectre de la rose* (1911) and to the eighteenth century, as in *The Sleeping Princess*, was really in love with the gorgeous East, as he showed in *Cléopâtre* (1909), *Scheherazade* (1910) and *Le Dieu bleu* (1912), and to a lesser extent with ancient Greece, which he evoked in *Narcisse* (1911), *L'Après-midi d'un faune* and *Daphnis et Chloë* (both 1913). The daring of his colour schemes was unparalleled. He was also one of the most fertile inventors of pattern who ever lived. These qualities, together with his eroticism, created a sensation in the West, made him as famous as Pavlova and Nijinsky, and caused a revolution in fashion and house decoration.

In 1914 for the first time Diaghilev employed a Moscow painter, Nathalie Gontcharova, whose brightly coloured peasant patterns, drawn with childish exaggeration, made the opera-ballet *Coq d'or* an overwhelming experience and revealed a new aspect of Russian-ness. Her husband Mikhail Larionov, whose passion for experiment was boundless, designed *Contes russes* (1918) in a similar exaggerated folk style, then in the remarkable *Chout* (1921), which he also helped to choreograph, combined ideas derived from Cubism, Delaunay's Orphism and Russian Rayonnism in tumultuous stage pictures. Dancers found his distorted wired and asymmetrical costumes difficult to perform in. *Renard* (1921 and 1929) was his last work for Diaghilev.

From 1917 onwards Diaghilev's designers were drawn increasingly from the School of Paris. In the historic *Parade* (1917) Picasso mixed stylised classical ballet costumes, a modern outfit bought at a big Paris store, and fantastic Cubist structures, which were less costumes than symbols of cities or civilizations. Picasso's *Tricorne* (1919) was a brilliant essay in eighteenth-century *pastiche* with a Spanish slant: it influenced stage designers for years to come. Against his Cubist Bay of Naples for *Pulcinella* (1920) he placed realistic costumes. Those for his genuine Spanish Gypsies in *Cuadro Flamenco* (1921), however, like those of *Le Tricorne*, were *appliqués* not only with bold patterns but with lines to suggest creases. While Derain brought his talents to bear on *La Boutique fantasque* (1919) and *Jack-in-the-Box* (1926), Matisse produced even more exquisite colour schemes and more slapdash simplified patterns for his *chinoiserie* in *Le Chant du Rossignol* (1920) a danced reduction of the Stravinsky opera for which Benois had made elaborate designs in 1914. Nothing could have been subtler than Braque's *chic* muddy colours for *Les Fâcheux* (1924), though the dressmaker must have found his drawings very hard to interpret. In *Zephire et Flore* (1925), an attempt to transform his delicate drawings of Muses (which were like a modern version of the drawings on Greek vases) into stylized modern dresses was unsuccessful. Certain painters who

could provide without difficulty pleasing and useful decors – and Laurencin, Utrillo and Rouault painted recognizable Laurencins, Utrillos and Rouaults for Diaghilev – found themselves at a loss to devise costumes which were both becoming and practical, and had to be helped out by dressmakers (such as Vera Sudeikina, later Mme Stravinsky) or members of Diaghilev's staff (such as Boris Kochno) or by Diaghilev himself.

As the 1920s advanced Diaghilev's hunger for experiment drove him to commission designs from the dressmaker Chanel, who made the costumes for *Le Train bleu* (1924) in a setting by the Cubist sculptor Laurens, from the Surrealists Ernst and Miró, who designed *Romeo and Juliet* (1926), from the Soviet Constructivist Yakulov, who designed the clanging factory of *Le Pas d'acier* (1927), from the non-representational sculptor Gabo, who fashioned a set and costumes out of gleaming plastic for *La Chatte* (1927), from the above mentioned Tchelitchev, whose white-clad dancers in *Ode* (1928) were the first ever to appear against cinematic projections, and from Chirico, the dreamer of empty arcaded squares and faceless statues, who designed *Le Bal* (1929).

Although for twenty years, in spite of war, revolution and lack of money, Diaghilev imposed his company as *the* Ballet of the western world, Rolf de Maré, a rich Swede, anxious to promote the dancer and choreographer Jean Borlin, briefly threatened his monopoly. In 1923 Les Ballets Suédois presented *La Création du monde*, designed by the Cubist Léger; in 1924 *Relâche*, designed by the Dadaist Picabia. A short-lived venture sponsored by Comte Etienne de Beaumont in 1924 occasioned, in Picasso's *Mercure*, one daring experiment. This Diaghilev later took over.

The Post-Diaghilev Period, 1929–1939: Ballet in the Melting Pot

The plan for Boris Kochno, Diaghilev's right-hand man and librettist, to carry on his company after Diaghilev's death in August, 1929, was defeated. Nevertheless Kochno initiated some of the best ballets to be made in the next few years. In 1932 Les Ballets de Monte Carlo, organized by René Blum and Colonel de Basil, reunited the talents of Diaghilev's régisseur, Grigoriev, of his choreographers Massine and Balanchine, of Boris Kochno and of some of his principal dancers. Three fine ballets devised by Kochno in 1932 were *Jeux d'enfants*, designed by Miró, *Cotillon* designed by Bérard, and *Concurrence*, designed by Derain. These ballets revealed to the world three 'baby ballerinas' discovered in the Russian émigré schools of Paris. When Kochno and Balanchine left Blum and de Basil, Edward James's Ballets 1933 gave them employment. Balanchine's *Errante*, designed by Tchelitchev, was admired by the young American Lincoln Kirstein, fresh from Harvard, and was one of the reasons which, against all reason, spurred him to carry off Balanchine to the New World, where ballet was almost unknown and certainly unwanted. In Europe Massine embarked on his first essays in 'symphonic ballet', *Présages* to the Fifth Symphony of Tchaikovsky and *Choreartium*, to the Fourth Symphony of Brahms, which were acclaimed as a sensational new departure; and their 'interpretation' of famous scores in terms of more-or-less classical dance, no less than their inconspicuous costumes, can now be seen as pointing forward to more subtle 'symphonic' works of Balanchine in future years.

There were several regroupings. In 1936 de Basil parted from Blum and founded a troupe which took his own name, while Blum directed another Ballets Russes de Monte Carlo. Then, in 1938, Massine too left de Basil, but not before he had created his *Symphonie fantastique* (1936), an essay in all-out Romanticism designed by Bérard. De Basil's Australian tour of 1938 prepared the way for the establishment of an Australian ballet company. Blum next called on Fokine to create *L'Epreuve d'amour* (1936), designed by Derain, and *Don Juan*, (1936), designed by Andreu, while Massine created Beethoven's *Seventh Symphony* (1938). There were further shuffles, law-suits and changes of name both before and after the outbreak of war, which exiled both semi-Russian companies to North and South America.

How can we summarize this chaotic period from the point of view of design? There was a tendency to employ artists who had worked for Diaghilev, such as Derain, Miró, Chirico, Tchelitchev, Matisse, Gontcharova or Soudeikine; and at least one new attempt was made to follow Diaghilev's example in luring a famous easel painter to design for the stage: Dufy designed *Beach* in 1933. The one outstanding new talent, promoted by Kochno, was that of Christian Bérard, designer not only of Balanchine's *Cotillon*, but of Massine's Berlioz and Beethoven symphonies.

In the plain all-over tights, with minimal accessories, which he used for *The Seventh Symphony*, Bérard followed the new trend towards a simpler ballet costume. Yet his *Cotillon*, dressed less simply, is remembered as the most miraculous (and perhaps typical) ballet of the 1930s. Its white marbled ballroom with red-curtained boxes belonged to no particular period, although the scarlet, yellow and emerald-green tail-coats of the men and the star-sprinkled bouffant skirts of the girls implied a hunt ball (around 1860?) attended only by aesthetes.

It was generally assumed that ballet meant Russian ballet – although some of Diaghilev's composers, designers and dancers had been French, Spanish, Italian or English. But the ex-Diaghilev dancer Marie Rambert had founded the Ballet Club in London in 1931; and the foundation of the Camargo Society (1930) was followed in 1931 by the installation of another ex-Diaghilev dancer, Ninette de Valois (who had previously provided dances

for operas and plays at the Old Vic), at the newly reopened Sadler's Wells Theatre. The Sadler's Wells Ballet, which Ashton left Rambert to join in 1935, after difficult years of competing unsuccessfully with the Russian companies, suddenly achieved popularity during the war, was established at Covent Garden in 1946, and in 1956 became the Royal Ballet.

In the early days, with no money to spare, both Rambert and de Valois had to look for designers in the highways and byways – or under the bed. Just as Rambert was impelled to turn a succession of dancers into choreographers – Ashton, Salaman, Tudor, Howard, Gore and Staff – so she discerned among some of her dancers – Salaman, Chappell, Howard and Laing – a talent for design. John Armstrong, a school-of-Picasso painter, designed Ashton's *Façade* (1931), while another young Englishman, Hugh Stevenson, made the first decors for Tudor's *Jardin aux Lilas* (1936), and Nadia Benois, niece of Alexandre, designed Tudor's *Dark Elegies* (1937), and Howard's *Lady into Fox* (1939). However, the designer who must rank as Rambert's chief gift to the world – and to Frederick Ashton – was the expatriate Russian, Sophie Fedorovitch, who might well be called England's Bérard. She designed Ashton's first ballet, *A Tragedy of Fashion* (1926), his *Masques* (1933), *Nocturne* (1937), and *Horoscope* (1938); and Howard's *Fête Etrange* (1940). Later she worked with Ashton at Covent Garden.

The Camargo Society had called on Vanessa Bell to design *Pomona* in 1930. For the Sadler's Wells Ballet Duncan Grant designed *The Enchanted Grove*, and Edward Burra, a less famous painter at that time, executed both *Rio Grande* (1931) and *Barabau* (1936). In 1935 Rex Whistler was invited by de Valois to design *The Rake's Progress*. In 1936 Cecil Beaton designed his first ballet (apart from a short number, *The First Shoot*, in a Cochran revue) for Ashton: this was the Romantic *Apparitions*. In 1937 the celebrated poster designer, E. McKnight Kauffer worked on *Checkmate* for de Valois.

By 1939, therefore, it could be said that pioneering English directors had summoned to the service of ballet, as Diaghilev had done, a few artists famous in another field. They had not, however, found employment for Sickert, for Augustus John (though a try had been made), for Matthew Smith or Stanley Spencer, each of whom, one might have thought, had at least one good ballet inside him. On the other hand, three designers destined for fame had made their debuts on the ballet scene: Fedorovitch, Whistler and Beaton. The fourth outstanding English designer of the day, Oliver Messel, whose all-white *Helen* (Offenbach's *Belle Hélène*), commissioned by C.B. Cochran, caused a sensation in 1932, had designed *Francesca da Rimini* (1938) for de Basil, but had not yet worked for an English ballet company.

Meanwhile, in France, Serge Lifar, whose flair for publicity was greater than his choreographic gift, but who

18TH-CENTURY PASTICHE (by the two Cubist painters). Georges Braque. Design for the Dance Maniac (Nijinska) in *Les Fâcheux*. © A.D.A.G.P. Paris, 1981. *Department of Prints & Drawings, V & A*

nevertheless inspired a younger generation by his enthusiasm for the art of ballet, was installed at the Paris Opéra, where he initiated a new régime.

In 1934 the American School of Ballet had been founded in New York, and Balanchine had made his first American ballet, *Serenade*.

Notes on some English designers

Of easel painters Edward Burra was by far the most talented to be employed for ballet: he was always successful in providing what was dramatically helpful without sacrificing his idiosyncratic quality as a painter. I never saw Ashton's *Rio Grande* (1932), but Constant Lambert's spicy score should make it well worth reviving. For Helpmann's *Miracle in the Gorbals* (1944), which had a magnificent threatening drop curtain representing the Glasgow docks, he gave a subtle twist to the modern clothes of his dockers and housewives, and integrated

them in his murky stage picture. Yet neither this ballet, not his even more ambitious *Don Quixote* (1950) for de Valois has survived.

Rex Whistler's charm and humour, as well as his early death in the Normandy landings, have caused a cult to grow up around him. An old-fashioned painter, he had an exceptional talent for book illustration, and his mock-eighteenth-century drawings in pen and ink were his most original inventions. Diaghilev would have valued these as decorations for *The World of Art*. Whistler's feeling for period style, as intense almost as that of Benois, made him an outstanding stage designer. Not only his front curtain for de Valois's *The Rake's Progress* (1935) with the perspective of an eighteenth-century street (I always remember a puddle among the cobbles) and his simplified monochrome sets after Hogarth, but his delicately coloured costumes retain their fascination.

Both Oliver Messel and Cecil Beaton admired Rex Whistler, their friend and contemporary; but neither had his knowledge of architecture and perspective. Both were better at designing costumes than sets.

The Sleeping Beauty of 1946, with which Sadler's Wells Ballet reopened Covent Garden after the war, was Messel's big opportunity. He remembered the Bakst production of 1921 and was determined to outdo it – not by heightening the colours or magnifying the splendour, which would have been impossible, but by giving rein to his power of poetic evocation. His baroque Never-Never Land was seen through veils of rococo, Romantic, Edwardian and 1920s nostalgia. The architectural sets were inspired by Watteau and the Bibiena family, but they were made to appear dreamlike and insubstantial – which helped to camouflage their shaky perspective. His costume designs needed 'interpretation' (his own word). Little touches of colour had to be evolved into patches of *appliqué* or embroidery. His headdresses – indeed all his props – realized by the fairy fingers of Hugh Skillen, were masterpieces of cobweb jewellery. He supervised the construction of these with maternal care. Sometimes an audacious combination of colour – pink with vermilion – came off: sometimes I thought him unable to detect a strident note – such as the too violent blue of the Bluebird's feathered costume. In 1946 certain dissonances could be blamed on the post-war shortage of good materials, on coupons and the ubiquity of rayon. When Messel's production was recreated for American Ballet Theatre in 1976 it was disastrously 'interpreted'. (I think there are no scene painters in New York as good as Harker in London).

Beaton, likewise, could occasionally get drunk with colour, as his costumes for *Turandot* will testify: but opera

18TH-CENTURY PASTICHE (by two Cubist painters). Pablo Picasso. Design for the Dandy (Idzikovsky) in *Le Tricorne*. © S.P.A.D.E.M. Paris, 1981. *Theatre Museum, V & A*

MODERN DRESS.
Chanel. Sokolova,
Dolin, Nijinska and
Woizikovsky in *Le
Train Bleu*. *Photo:
Sasha (left)*

MODERN DRESS.
Leon Bakst, Serge
Diaghilev and
Paquin (who all had
a hand in the
designs). Nijinsky,
Karsavina and
Schollar in *Jeux*.

MODERN DRESS.
Kermit Love. Eckl.
Kidd, Kriza and
Robbins in *Fancy
Free*. *Photo: Baron*

ROBERTH NORTH "STAGES"

Contemporary dance theatre. — Farmer

MODERN DRESS. Peter Farmer. Design for the Hero (Robert North) in *Stages. Theatre Museum, V & A*

near the hem of the skirt with tinselly flowers or masks. To this picture Beaton wished to give a mother-of-pearl iridescence by patches of blue, pink and green light. He had a genius for costume design and could have made his fortune as a dressmaker. A dandy himself, he knew so well what was becoming to men or women, and usually curbed his fantasy before it went too far. In the remarkable Ascot scene of *My Fair Lady*, though it was all in black and white, he *did* deliberately go too far, but then this dress parade was treated as a crazy slow-motion ballet, and the hats and dresses of 1910 had undergone a Beardsleyesque metamorphosis. The challenge of working with Boris Kochno for the Ballets des Champs-Elysées on *Devoirs de vacances* (1949) and with Lincoln Kirstein for New York City Ballet on *Illuminations* (1950), brought out some of his most imaginative costumes, even if those for Fonteyn and Nureyev in *Marguerite and Armand* (1963) achieved wider fame. Like his dresses for *Apparitions*, the latter were *pastiches* of the Romantic period.

Ashton preferred self-effacing designers, and Sophie Fedorovitch suited him well – although her most perfect work, *La Fête Etrange* (1940), was designed for another, Andrée Howard. This wintry masquerade, in which Fedorovitch's simple, subtly coloured costumes shone against the merest suggestion of a formal French garden under snow, exactly matching the melancholy airs of Fauré, was one of the best English ballets. Postwar ballets designed by her for Ashton at Covent Garden and Sadler's Wells were *Symphonic Variations* (1946) and *Valses Nobles et Sentimentales* (1947). But Ashton did not employ Fedorovitch when he turned to making three-act ballets. Of these the most popular and the most likely to endure was *La Fille mal gardée* (1960), but its designs by the cartoonist Osbert Lancaster were uninspired; Lancaster's urban rather than pastoral muse was the 'spirit of place' – as shown in the Bayswater set for Cranko's *Bonne Bouche* (1952) and the Portsmouth quayside in Cranko's *Pineapple Poll* (1951) – but his costumes for Ashton's comic ballet, as for *Coppélia* (1954) were conventional. (*Coppélia* tended to bring out the worst in British designers – among whom I include the Australian Loudon Sainthill.) Ashton certainly tried to employ a few British painters from beyond the narrow pale of stage decorators: for instance both George Sheringham and Derek Hill designed his *Lord of Burleigh* in 1932 and 1937, Graham Sutherland designed his *Wanderer* of 1941, John Piper his *Quest* of 1943, John Craxton his *Daphnis and Chloë* of 1951, and Isabel Lambert his *Tiresias* of 1951 and his *Madame Chrysantème* of 1955, but the results were not memorable. Nor did his collab-

does not concern us here. His ballroom in *Apparitions* (1936) was all white and poetically conceived: on the plain white flats only the shadow of a chandelier or a 'cello appeared. The men's tail-coats were coloured but all the girls' ball dresses were white and trimmed on one side

MODERN DRESS. Edward Burra. Designs for Old Woman of the Gorbals and Sauchiehall Street. Girl in *Miracle in the Gorbals. Theatre Museum, V & A*

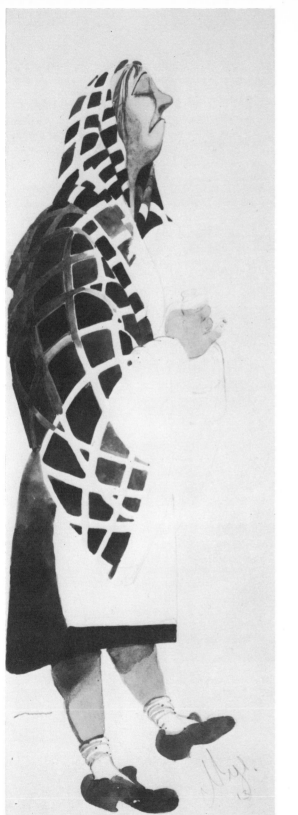

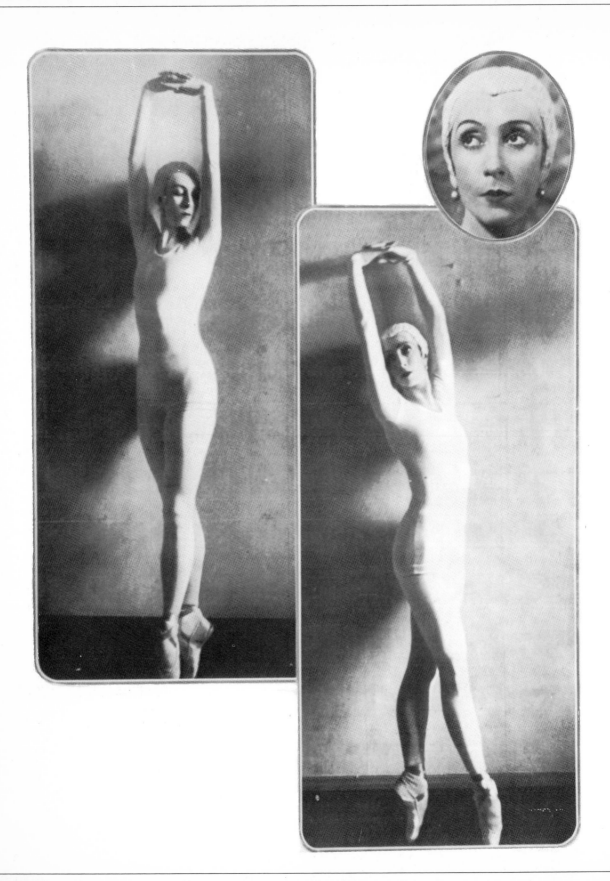

QUASI-NUDITY.
Pavel Tchelitchev.
Doubrovska in *Ode*.
Photo: Lipnitzki
(left)

QUASI-NUDITY.
Pavel Tchelitchev.
The male corps de
ballet in *Ode*. *Photo:
Lipnitzki*

QUASI-NUDITY.
Joan Mirò.
Toumanova,
Eglevsky and
Rostova in *Jeux
d'enfants*. *Photo:
Raoul Barba*

orations with designers from Paris, such as André Beaurepaire in *Scènes de Ballet* (1948), Jean-Denis Malclès in *Cinderella* (1948), Lila de Nobili in *Ondine* (1958) or Jacques Dupont in *The Two Pigeons* (1961) have entirely happy results. This may have been the fault of Covent Garden's scene-painters and dressmakers. One could see, for instance, that the talented de Nobili's designs for the ballroom in *Ondine* were crudely interpreted, as were those of Dupont for the Messager ballet.

The morbid fancies of Leslie Hurry were first harnessed by Helpmann for *Hamlet* in 1942, and Hurry designed for the (Sadler's Wells) Royal Ballet no less than three productions of *Swan Lake*, the first in 1943. Helpmann also had the daring to employ his fellow Australian, Arthur Boyd, for *Elektra* in 1963.

Boyd, a visionary painter whose folklore was personal as Chagall's, had formerly, at my suggestion, designed a striking *Renard* for Western Theatre Ballet at Lord Harewood's first Edinburgh Festival of 1961. In the same programme of ballets with singing two other talented Australian designers were revealed. Ian Spurling, inspired by feverish visions of an Art Deco that never was on land or sea, designed *Seven Deadly Sins*. (His ingenious excesses tended in 1974 to swamp the humour of MacMillan's *Elite Syncopations* at Covent Garden.) Barry Kay, who designed a very pretty *Salade*, turned out a far more versatile designer, whose imagination could illuminate a diversity of themes.

Two other gifted Australians must be named: Kenneth Rowell, whose mineralogical decors for MacMillan's *Baiser de la Fée* (1960) were marvellous and new; and Sidney Nolan, who is also the most celebrated living Australian painter. Commissioned by MacMillan to design a new version of *The Rite of Spring* (1962), Nolan dressed his primitive celebrants in all-over tights which were intended to suggest the paint-daubed bodies of naked aboriginals.

From the start Kenneth MacMillan showed an adventurous policy with regard to design; and having discovered an artist who delivered the goods he stuck to him. The Greek-born, but later naturalised, Nicholas Georgiadis, gave us a new kick even with his earliest designs for *House of Birds* and *Danses Concertantes* (both 1955) which were a little influenced by Jackson Pollock's dripping paint; he then designed *The Invitation* (1961), an important ballet in which simplified 1910 costumes contrasted with almost – but not quite – abstract sets; and went on to plan such huge productions as *Romeo and Juliet* (1965), *Manon* (1974) and *Mayerling* (1978). He had begun as an abstract painter, and I always felt he first assembled his masses of colour and his forms, then began to grope his way towards the delineation of an identifiable locality or a costume in period style, but stopped – as Romney is said to have stopped when he saw a likeness coming – before an excess of detail could overlay his initial scheme.

This is a very good way of setting about things. Georgiadis's colour sense is sure and he has proved the most original designer of the last decades. He also designed Nureyev's *Nutcracker* (1968), *Swan Lake* (not yet seen in England) and *The Sleeping Beauty* (Milan, 1966, restaged for the Festival Ballet, 1975). Himself a pupil of Iannis Tsarouchis (one of the greatest living painters and a stage designer whose poetic imagination and wide range the English have hardly been able to judge from productions of the opera *Medea* and *The Birds* of Aristophanes), Georgiadis has since taught stage design at the Slade School, guiding a new generation of talented designers. Among these are Yolanda Sonnabend, Stefanos Lazaridis and Peter Docherty (also Bernard Culshaw, whose chief work has been for Kent Opera).

It was Barry Kay who created *Anastasia* (1970) for MacMillan. His sets with their double meanings – a ship was a birch forest, a ballroom became a revolutionary barricade – were superb, but he was hampered, as Georgiadis was in *Mayerling* (1975) by the choreographer's decision to put on stage a court (Russian or Austrian) dressed in realistic costumes.

Both Georgiadis and Kay designed wonderful productions of *The Sleeping Beauty*. That of the former, for Nureyev and Festival Ballet (1975), though built to tour, had Louis XIV costumes of heartening splendour; Georgiadis's red, black and gold *ballet de cour*, ingeniously arranged by Nureyev to open the final act, showed an almost miraculous insight into the nature of these courtly spectacles described by Dr Strong in his preceding essay, and which were born from a belief in the Divine Right of Kings. Kay's *Sleeping Beauty*, made for the Berlin Opera House (1967), began at the court of Catherine the Great, with gold against gold, and ended, when Aurora had been awoken from her hundred-years sleep, with uniforms of the period of Alexander III, and Jewel Fairies like Fabergé Easter eggs.

I have mentioned the inhibiting effect of realistic costume. Yet after the early 1960s when ballet tried to follow the lead of John Bury and the Royal Shakespeare Company, when painted sets were looked on askance, when scenery was built of stark wood or iron and costumes were limited to the virile armour of leather and metal, all colour being banned, there were signs of a reaction in favour of realism. Ashton was one choreographer who evidently yearned for a return to delicacy and detail; and the almost photographic *verismo* of Zeffirelli's productions of *Cav* and *Pag* in 1959 perhaps influenced Julia Trevelyan Oman's loving reconstructions of Edwardian England in Ashton's *Enigma Variations* (1968) and of Tchekhovian Russia in his *A Month in the Country* (1975). Elgar's watch-chain and the piano on which Chopin was played were the genuine article, and every autumn leaf was discernibly beech or birch.

Alexandre Benois design for the Ballerina (Karsavina) in *Petrushka. Theatre Museum, V & A*

Natalia Gontcharova design for a peasant in *Le Coq d'or.* © A.D.A.G.P. Paris, 1981. *Department of Prints and Drawings, V & A*

Nicholas Georgiadis designs for the Husband and the Wife in *The Invitation. Theatre Museum, V & A*

Pablo Picasso design for the Miller in *Le Tricorne.* © S.P.A.D.E.M. Paris, 1981. *Theatre Museum, V & A*

Giorgio di Chirico costume for *Le Bal*. © *Sunday Times* Photo: *David Montgomery*

Sophie Fedorovitch design for Guests in *La Fête étrange*. *Theatre Museum, V & A*

Top right:
Jean Hugo design for characters in *Les Amours de Jupiter*. *Artist's collection*

Lower right:
Oliver Messel costumes of Catalabutte (Edwards), Queen (Bedells) and King (Davenport) from the *Sleeping Beauty*. *Photo: Frank Sharman*

Les décors de ballet d'Enrico Prampolini. Maquette de ballet.

Robert Rauschenberg costumes for *Summerspace*. Photo: *Jack Mitchell*

Yet such realism was not in the spirit of the age; nor were three-act ballets; nor was Ashton's hankering for the past. Ashton could, however, make dances without the trimmings of costume, comedy or characterization, and which stirred the soul as powerfully as a work by Balanchine. My own favourite among his works, *Monotones* (1966), was performed in white all-over tights.

It was Norman Morrice, when he worked for Ballet Rambert, who discovered Ralph Koltai, a designer with a stark, new approach. His costumes, though, were usually designed by Nadine Baylis. *She* is the heir of Tchelitchev; and has invented more ways of being nude than any other living designer. By 'being nude', as I have indicated above, I do not mean dispensing with jockstrap and bra. In Tetley's *Ziggurat* (1967) Baylis dressed her dancers in holes.

Notes on some French Designers of the 1940s

The installation of Lifar as *maître de ballet* at the Paris Opéra, although he reanimated the ballet company of that Byzantine institution, produced no durable works of art. Among the designers he employed were Léger, who had worked for the Ballets Suédois, and Cassandre, whose posters Diaghilev had admired, and who had designed Balanchine's handsome *Aubade* for the Ballets de Monte Carlo in 1936. These two created for Lifar respectively *David Triomphant* (1937) and *Le Chevalier et la Demoiselle* (1941).

The renaissance of ballet design in France followed the liberation of Paris, and was entirely due to Boris Kochno, who founded the Ballets des Champs-Elysées with the young choreographer Roland Petit in 1945. No one who was present when this company opened at the Adelphi in London in April 1946 will forget the joyous occasion. The sunburst of French genius after the dark years of war was as shining a revelation as must the Diaghilev Ballet have been to the London of 1918. There seemed to be a different designer of outstanding talent for every work.

Bérard was remembered, of course, but his *Les Forains* was a new masterpiece of simplicity. Not only the set – a black void against which the strolling players erected two poles and a shabby red curtain, brought to magical life by the switching on of a light – but the elementary costumes of the Conjuror, the Sleeping Beauty, the Acrobat and the Siamese Twins, made an indelible impression. In a later ballet of Bérard's, *La Rencontre, ou Oedipe et le Sphinx* (1948), with choreography by Lichine, the action took place in a deserted circus ring in the desolate outskirts of Thebes, and, as I wrote 'Young Leslie Caron in white all-over tights and claws was the Sphinx . . . part beautiful woman, part acrobat, part monster. Her lair was a red velvet trapeze in mid-air; her wings, originally conceived by Bérard as feathery and angelic, were simplified to

mere lengths of white material which were drawn upwards into two triangles when she put her riddles.'

'White all-over tights' with the distinguishing additions of a symbolic head-dress or a minimal draped cloak or scarf were also the uniform of both gods and mortals in *Les Amours de Jupiter* (1946), designed by Jean Hugo for Kochno and Petit; and it is noteworthy that, although Balanchine was far away beyond the Atlantic, the two greatest of French designers, Bérard and Hugo, were still in the main line of development, which I have designated as the spirit of the age. Apart from such plays as Cocteau's *Orphée*, Racine's *Phèdre* and Victor Hugo's *Ruy Blas*, Hugo had designed one ballet, *Les Cent Baisers* (1935), for de Basil; and *Jupiter* was to be his last, for he became disenchanted by theatrical compromise. The white-clad Europa, carried off across a black and ancient sea, the white-clad Ganymede borne into the azure, and the white-clad Danaë in her terra-cotta octagon, with legs quivering to receive the shower of gold, remain haunting images.

Did Jean Cocteau's garret for *Le Jeune Homme et la Mort* (1946), 'dictated to Georges Wakhevitch', and the paint-smeared overalls he ordained for Jean Babilée, set the fashion for squalid, peeling walls, patched with newspaper, and for rags and tatters, which we associated, perhaps arbitrarily, with the new and hardly understood philosophy, existentialism? Stanislas Lepri's *Le Bal des blanchisseuses* (1946) and Léonor Fini's *Les Demoiselles de la nuit* (1948), the latter made for Roland Petit's Ballets de Paris after Petit had broken with Kochno, belonged, with their *nostalgie de la boue*, in this neo-romantic category.

Rags and tatters! Ragged drapery, a tattered lace curtain, common wooden chairs, wheels, ladders, and a rickety iron bed, were the *objets trouvés* which furnished the scenes of *Carmen* (1949), designed by Antoni Clavé for Petit's Ballets de Paris, and which contrived, no less than the props of Bérard's *Forains*, to make a virtue out of poverty. With her short hair, black corset and endless white legs, Jeanmaire appeared *plus nue que le nu*; and Clavé's huge splashes of colour sang out of limbo. He was an entirely original and an entirely successful designer, who flashed comet-like across the sky of ballet between 1946 and 1957 and then was heard of no more. His one ballet for England was *Ballabile*, staged by Petit at Covent Garden in 1950. His earliest had been an excursion into the Spain of Goya, *Los Caprichos* (1946); and of course it was Boris Kochno who had given him that first chance.

André Beaurepaire, another original, who designed *Concert de Danses* (1946) for the Champs-Elysées, had the mind of a demented prince bred in the prisons of Piranesi, whose visions both Gothic and baroque nevertheless anticipated the discovery of America. His bejewelled ballerina wore a *diamanté* Balinese helmet. It was I who brought Beaurepaire to London to design Ashton's *Scènes*

QUASI-NUDITY. George Balanchine. Farrell and Martins in *Agon*.
Photo: Martha Swope

QUASI-NUDITY. Nadine Baylis. Dancers in *Ziggurat*. *Photo: Anthony Crickmay (right)*

Alexandre Benois. Design for Aristocratic Children in *Petrushka*. *Theatre Museum, V & A*

de ballet (1948), his set for which was like the ruins of a prehistoric railway staion.

Kochno could conjure masterly designers out of thin air. Tom Keogh's *Portrait de Don Quichotte* (1947) and *Till Eulenspiegel* (1949) were reminiscent both of Beardsley and Bérard, with colours shrill as candy. Nor can Christian Dior's *Treize Danses* (1948) he forgotten.

After the disappearance of the Ballets des Champs-Elysées and the Ballets de Paris, the French scene was dominated by Le Grand Ballet du Marquis de Cuevas, run by this charming Chilean dilettante on his (Rockefeller) wife's American money, and which, though based on Paris, toured the world. Yet of all the ballets staged by this expansive troupe in the 1940s and 1950s, only one springs to mind, Taras's *Piège de Lumière* (1952), with its fantastic butterfly costumes of André Levasseur.

The French tradition of employing distinguished painters for ballet was continued by the Ballet Théâtre Contemporain (founded 1968), whose decor for Stravinsky's *Rossignol* by Tuan was outstanding, and by Petit, who, in the sixties had recourse to Nicky Saint-Phalle and Martial Raisse.

Notes on some American designers since 1933

We have observed above how Tchelitchev arrived in New York shortly after Balanchine. Lincoln Kirstein, having established with the latter the American School of Ballet, was desperately trying to find outlets for his Messiah of choreography. In May 1936, with three soloists and a handful of dancers, Gluck's *Orpheus* was staged by

Balanchine and Tchelitchev as an opera-ballet at the Metropolitan Opera House, the singers being banished to the pit. The Orpheus of Lew Christensen was 'a big boy in a transparent T-shirt and black trunks . . . both athlete and poet. Across his back was strung a crystal lyre.' Thus Kirstein. 'In the final scene, spread across a wide sky was a self-illuminated Milky Way, thousands of stars . . . within this vast surround there were only three figures . . . performing a deliberate interlace at once intensely erotic and plastically splendid . . . The result was the most beautiful visual spectacle I have seen on the stage.' This historic production was given only twice. 'The general responses were titters, yawns, or weak ironic applause . . . The omnipotent music critic of the *New York Times* found it all "absurd".'

Tchelitchev designed *Nobilissima Visione* for Massine (1938); and in 1941 Balanchine's *Balustrade* for de Basil's Original Ballet Russe, which had three performances only, in Brooklyn. The Theatre Museum is lucky to possess five costumes for this ballet to Stravinsky's Violin Concerto, including Toumanova's extraordinary black fish-net bodice, with a jewelled *parure* which Wilde's

Natalia Gontcharova. Designs for women dancers in *Les Noces*. © A.D.A.G.P. Paris, 1981. Department of Prints & Drawings, V & A

Herodias might have envied, and gloves from whose finger-tips drip pear-shaped emeralds and rubies. Other costumes, patterned with leafy veins, can be related to the artist's *Hide and Seek* in the Museum of Modern Art – which owns incidentally, the designs for *Orpheus*. After two further collaborations with Balanchine in Buenos Aires in 1942, *Apollon Musagète* and *Concerto*, Tchelitchev worked no more for the stage. It was as if he had pointed the way, then left Balanchine and Kirstein to carry on.

While Kirstein battled with every conceivable adversity, including a world war – during which he took a small troupe, Ballet Caravan, on a tour of Latin America before joining the armed forces – the expatriate Russian-Monte-Carlo companies, continually changing names and intentions, and exchanging choreographers, dancers and sponsors, milled around the Americas. The impresario Sol Hurok, who booked all tours, held the key to a company's survival in the United States, though never to anyone's solvency but his own: and he believed ballet was inevitably Russian.

Yet out of this confusion a famous company, American Ballet Theatre, was born in 1940. Lucia Chase, an able ex-pupil of Mordkin (Pavlova's one-time partner) was its director and secret backer; and enlisted the support of the designer Oliver Smith. From the start Ballet Theatre's policy was eclectic. It would embrace the old repertoires of Diaghilev and de Basil, and employ Fokine, Massine

and Balanchine to stage new works. When the war brought England's Antony Tudor, Markova and Dolin to America it would employ them too; but it would also, in spite of Hurok, encourage local talent, commissioning American choreographers and designers. This looked fine on paper; and variety added spice to programmes calculated to whet the appetite of a new and innocent audience: but the troupe suffered from having no single choreographer of talent to take control and forge a style for it. The repertory was too haphazard.

Among the most successful new works created by Ballet Theatre in its early years were Tudor's *Pillar of Fire* (1942), designed by Jo Mielziner, who was already famous on Broadway, Agnes de Mille's *Rodeo* (1942) (which was an ancestor of the musical *Oklahoma!*), with set by Oliver Smith and costumes by Saul Bolasni, and Robbins's *Fancy Free* (1944) (which was blown up into the musical *On the Town*), with set by Oliver Smith and costumes by Kermit Love. Eugene Loring's *Billy the Kid* (1938), designed by Jared French, was taken over from Kirstein's Ballet Caravan.

The mention of these native American works, the second and fourth of which had scores by Aaron Copland, the third by Leonard Bernstein, brings us to the problem of adapting modern dress to ballet. This became increasingly easy as the years went by. Nijinsky's tennis players in *Jeux* (1913) reflected the modern mania for sport; Chanel's bathing costumes in *Le Train bleu* (1924) illustrated the new fashion for exposing tender aristocratic flesh to the summer sun. Loring, De Mille and Robbins put cowboys and sailors on the stage. The costumes of neither demanded much reduction or simplification. From the 1950s onwards, as sweaters, T-shirts and jeans became an increasingly obligatory uniform for young people all over the world, so abstract, storyless or classical ballet, clad in more and more vestigial costumes, would appear less remote from the encounters and involvements of everyday life.

Two distinguished and very different designers who worked for Ballet Theatre may be mentioned. Eugene Berman (ex-Russia, ex-Paris) who created Tudor's ornate *Romeo and Juliet* (1943), conjuring up his personal vision of the Italian Renaissance, harked back to the courtly pageants of the Medici. Irene Sharaff, with her bright-coloured jerseys, tunics and trousers for Robbins's *Interplay* (1945) stood for the carefree if competitive New World, where dancing and athletics were *popular* spectacles.

In 1948 Kirstein and Balanchine, with a measure of municipal support, founded New York City Ballet. Did anyone quote Shelley: 'The world's great age begins anew,/The golden years return'? When the company came to Covent Garden in 1950, the English thought they had soulless choreography, too little scenery, and no male dancers. By the time they returned in 1979 they had

Giorgio di Chirico. Design for the two men in the Spanish *pas de trois* in *Le Bal*. © S.P.A.D.E.M. Paris, 1981. *Theatre Museum, V & A*

Giorgio di Chirico. Balanchine and Doubrovska in the Spanish *pas de trois* in *Le Bal*. Photo: Numa Blanc *(right)*

even less scenery, but a multitude of wonderful dancers, male and female, sprung from the School of American Ballet; and Balanchine's variety of invention was universally acclaimed. Yet a somewhat showy piece, *The Seasons* by Jerome Robbins, with some of the most vulgar costumes ever designed, was more loudly applauded. Things do change, but not entirely. In 1980 I watched with interest three programmes of the New York City Ballet in Paris. Now, the Parisians are notoriously avid for new visual sensations. There was no decor at all and the

Martha Graham. McGuire and Asakawa in *Diversion of Angels*.   Graham, Cohan and Ross in *Night Journey*. *(right)*
Photo: Martha Swope

minimum of costume, and yet the packed audience, many of whom had paid £25 a seat, were perfectly satisfied. To this extent had Balanchine, giving not a damn for anybody, imposed his new kind of ballet.

Kirstein could appreciate what Balanchine was doing in the sphere of pure dance better than the next man – indeed he had given up his life to make Balanchine's achievement possible, and the Stravinsky-Balanchine ballets which have been a peak of twentieth century art were either commissioned or promoted by him: but he was an aesthete like Diaghilev, and longed to involve painters (not to mention poets) in the business of making ballets. Yet, when he produced a clever designer such as Kurt Seligmann for *The Four Temperaments* (1946), Joan Junyer for *The Minotaur* (1947) or Esteban Francès for *Till Eulenspiegel* (1951) and *A Figure in the Carpet* (1960), it was observed either that the costumes were quietly shed in favour of anonymous tights or that these decorated ballets were dropped from the repertory. An exception was the *Orpheus* designed by Isamu Noguchi. This remarkable sculptor had invented a new kind of exquisite three-dimensional scenery for Martha Graham's *Appalachian Spring* (1944), *Cave of the Heart* and *Night Journey* (both 1947), although the costumes for these had been either by Edythe Gilfond or by Graham herself: and in 1948 Noguchi designed both decor and costumes for the Stravinsky-Balanchine *Orpheus* with outstanding success.

When New York City Ballet needed *tutus* or conventional romantic ballet dresses, as opposed to plain tights, they came more and more to rely on the gifted dressmaker Barbara Karinska, designer of costumes for *Bourrée fantasque* (1949), *La Valse* (1951), *Stars and Stripes* (1958), *Liebeslieder Walzer* (1960), *Bugaku* (1963), and *Jewels* (1967): but her decors were perfunctory. For grander spectacles such as the revivals of *Nutcracker, Harlequinade* and *Coppelia* Kirstein called upon the many-sided and inventive Rouben Ter-Arutunian, whose glowing colours for the Chinese costumes of Taras's *Song of the Nightingale* (1972) really rivalled those of Bakst or Clavé. This designer also conceived the spare but impeccable sets and costumes for Glen Tetley's *Ricercare* and *Pierrot Lunaire*, both of which have been shown in England by the Ballet Rambert. In recent years Kirstein has left Balanchine increasingly to his own devices, with results that are not always happy. While the great choreographer understands all there is to be known about line, he has no sense of colour, and settles too readily for a combination of pastel pinks and blues.

Isamu Noguchi. Tallchief and Magallanes in *Orpheus. Photo: George Platt Lynes*

To Jerome Robbins is due the credit for luring the remarkable painter and graphic artist Ben Shahn, and the cartoonist Saul Steinberg to write for ballet. The former's *Opus Jazz* (1958) had costumes by Florence Klotz. For *The Concert* (1958) the latter designed a front curtain only; the costumes were by Irene Sharaff.

What of the Modern Dance? Like a Greek sculptor, Martha Graham preferred draperies for her women and nakedness for her men. In *Diversion of Angels* (1948) she herself had devised (perhaps in collaboration with Oliver Fray) a new way of cutting a skirt so that it left the legs as free almost as would trousers, yet which could be so voluminous as to cover the head like a cloak. This was a *trouvaille* as startling as that of Mme Vionnet, the Paris *couturière* of the 1930s, who invented dresses cut on the cross to mould more seductively the female torso. The crowns and hat-pins Noguchi designed for Graham are part of history. Like rocks in a Japanese garden, the mysterious symbolic objects which composed Noguchi's scenery depended on exact placing in relationship to each other. They also depended for the fulfilment of their joyous or tragic function on subtle lighting, and of this Jean Rosenthal was a master. With her magic hand on the controls no decor was necessary – although she later designed the transparent architecture of a dance studio for Robbins's *Afternoon of a Faun* (1953).

As a designer of sets, Noguchi was certainly amongst the most original who ever lived. I recall his non-representational but just-right Garden of Eden in *Embattled Garden* (1958), a sloping scarlet and green platform bristling with flexible metal poles, a machine in which to make love and hate. In *Seraphic Dialogue* (1955) a geometry of golden rods conveyed a Gothic cathedral, while the colours of its stained glass were supplied by the long plain robes of the dancers.

Merce Cunningham, Paul Taylor, Glen Tetley and Robert Cohan, the next generation of Modern choreographers, absorbed the lessons of Balanchine as well as those of Graham. As they fused the contractions of Graham, and her use of the floor, with the extensions and airy flights of classical ballet, so their costumes tended more and more to the Balanchinean ideal of quasi-nudity. In Cunningham's *Summerspace* (1958), which New York City Ballet took over, Robert Rauschenberg's sheeny silken tights were speckled with *pointilliste* rainbow dots like his backcloth. This was beautiful.

Whether the marvellous inventions of Alwin Nikolais come under the heading of dance costumes one is at liberty to doubt: for he has created a new heaven and a new earth, whose inhabitants, sometimes faceless, legless or armless, though sometimes with an extra joint to their arms ending in a plunger, are governed by no earthly laws – and indeed elastic often replaces gravity. His cornucopia of ideas could well be turned to the service of spectacles in which actual dancing plays a more vital part. No doubt, though, that in such works as *Imago, Group Dance* and *Noumenon*, choreography and design are totally merged.

A Ray of Hope for the Designer

Having shown, or tried to, that the designer has become a superfluous luxury, if not an encumbrance, in the ballet world of the 1980s, I should like to offer him a few crumbs of comfort.

I have remarked on Balanchine's lack of colour sense. Someone is needed to remedy such a deficiency. Tights and *tutus* cannot always be black and white. To make a perfect blend of three colours needs as much art as to design *Scheherazade*. Think how Robbins's *Dances at a Gathering* could have been improved if the shirts and tunics had been conceived in less sickly hues. Then, today's designer must be an accomplished dressmaker, for there are so many ways of getting the simplest costume wrong.

He must also be an artist in lighting, which has become more important than paint and nearly as important as music. Lighting electrifies the commonplace, like the poetry of Wordsworth or Cocteau. One of the most thrilling sets in my experience was designed by the American William Katz for Louis Falco's *Twopenny Portrait*, 'a sad-funny duet for two melancholy urban lovers', which we saw at Sadler's Wells. I wrote: 'Who would have thought that six or eight ribbed metal dustbins on an empty stage could be transformed by gentle coloured lighting into magic and monumental objects – a kind of slummy

Stonehenge for lost souls to wander in?' The designer-electrician must consider himself the heir not only of Jean Rosenthal, of Tchelitchev, of Diaghilev and of Loie Fuller, but of Monet, Turner, Vermeer and Caravaggio; and of course he must be thoroughly versed in the history of art.

Even in this age, which is ceasing to be modern as I write, he will from time to time be called upon to design great spectacles; for the classical ballets from *Giselle* to *The Sleeping Beauty* will always be revived: so he must have at his finger-tips the laws of perspective, architecture, anatomy and landscape painting, as well as a thorough knowledge of the styles and costumes of every country and every period. He must therefore be the master of more skills than any of his predecessors.

It is always salutary to reflect on pedigrees. Balanchine is not only the heir of Petipa but of a tradition going back beyond King Louis XIV, whose grandmother was a Medici, to the Florentine court where spectacular ballet may be said to have been born. The pedigree of our Royal Ballet is as traceable as our Queen's. Patronage today takes a new form, for the Arts Council, the Midland Bank and the Ford Foundation have replaced Grand Duke Cosimo I of Tuscany and his royal descendants in Paris and London. Yet Lincoln Kirstein went to Paris and London to fetch Balanchine, just as Inigo Jones went to Italy to learn his trade; and because of *both* these journeys the spirit of the Medici is alive in Manhattan.

Today's designer must see himself in relation to those Mannerist painters such as Vasari and Buontalenti, who could turn their hands to so many applied arts, of which stage decoration was only one. These men knew Michelangelo, who died two months before Shakespeare was born.

On Designing for Ballet Today

Barry Kay and Liz da Costa talk to
Alexander Schouvaloff, Curator of the Theatre Museum,
Victoria & Albert Museum

Barry Kay was born in Melbourne. He studied principally in Paris at the Académie Julien after which he moved to London where he has lived since 1956. His first designs seen with the Western Theatre Ballet resulted in a commission to design *Measure for Measure* at the Old Vic. Among the plays he has designed for the Royal Shakespeare Company are *Victor* by Vitrac and the John Schlesinger production of *No Why* by John Whiting. He has further collaborated on Schlesinger's film work as consultant designer.

For the opera his work includes Janacek's *The Cunning Little Vixen* with the Sadler's Wells Opera and the Solti/Hartmann production of *Die Meistersinger von Nürnberg* for the Royal Opera, Covent Garden.

After designing for the Royal Swedish Ballet and the Théâtre de la Monnaie, Barry Kay's first production for the Royal Ballet was *Images of Love* for Kenneth MacMillan in 1963. Since then they have been closely associated both in England and abroad. At the Deutsche Oper, Berlin, they collaborated on such ballets as *The Sleeping Beauty*

and *Anastasia* in 1967, followed by *Cain and Abel* in 1968. *Miss Julie* was designed for the Stuttgart Ballet in 1969 and the full-length version of *Anastasia* was produced for The Royal Ballet in 1971. More recently he has designed MacMillan's new production of *Solitaire* for the Sadler's Wells, Royal Ballet. Then for the Paris Opéra – *Metaboles* and *The Four Seasons* in 1978.

He has worked on a number of different versions of Rudolf Nureyev's *Don Quixote*, notably for the first production in 1966 at the Vienna State Opera and for the Australian Ballet Company in 1970. He returned to Australia in 1972 as production designer for the filming of this ballet which was also directed by Nureyev. Their work together includes *Raymonda* for The Royal Ballet in 1966 and *Tancredi* for the Vienna State Opera in that same year.

He is now working on *Isadora*, a new full length ballet by Kenneth MacMillan which commemorates the 50th anniversary of the founding of The Royal Ballet.

His stage designs are represented in the theatre collections of The British Council, the Theatre Museum, Victoria and Albert Museum, and numerous European, North American and Australian museum collections.

Barry Kay: I remember that my first real interest in the theatre was due to the Ballet Rambert Company which came to Australia when I was fifteen. I was enormously impressed. It was at a time when they had reached an especially high point artistically. This is what gave me my first thoughts about working in the theatre.

A S: Ballet in particular?

Barry Kay: Yes. At least at that stage. Until then my main preoccupation was music – piano and composition. I was interested in composition from very early on. From the age of fifteen I began to develop in a new direction – towards painting. So with a little persuasion my parents sent me to art college in Melbourne. It was not very long after that I managed to go to Paris to study painting at the Académie Julien. But for me the most exciting part soon became the theatre. This was Paris shortly after the war and it had burst forth with some of the most remarkable stage designing to have been seen since the Diaghilev era. It was from that moment that I really decided this was what I should do. The Ballet des Champs Elysées was the focal point with its productions by Roland Petit. I think it caught a lot of our imaginations. I believe that it did in the case of Kenneth MacMillan who felt a similar reaction at the time. I managed to see everything they did many times over. Also I met and came to know designers like Clavé and others, which in some ways helped more than the academic work I was being taught at school.

I then returned to Australia for a short time and began

working with Walter Gore, who had formed a company out there with his wife Paula Hinton. I designed several ballets for them which really gave me a basis for the work I was to commence in Europe.

A S: Why didn't you want to stay in Australia?

Barry Kay: Because I felt there was very little further advancement I could make in the Australian theatre. What I had seen in France had left a great impression and the Australian theatre seemed both dull and limited; not what it has become today.

Besides, there was an unfortunate snobbery about local talent which denied progress to those who had not travelled or achieved success abroad. It's not that I particularly responded to that pressure but I needed to develop in a more demanding climate. It seemed that the only way that I could hope to expand, was to go abroad.

This is how I came to London where I worked for a short time with the Western Theatre Ballet, a very interesting and adventurous small company. This followed with plays which I designed for the Old Vic and the Royal Shakespeare Company. Around this time I met Kenneth MacMillan with whom I have since had a close partnership in designing many of his ballets. It has been a considerable influence on my work.

A S: What do you mean by 'a close partnership' between designer and choreographer?

Barry Kay: Well it doesn't always happen. I think it is something which develops through a long period of working together. The approach has to be complementary so that each one knows the direction in which the other is going without necessarily having to say it. I have always experienced this with MacMillan and also with Nureyev. Such a working partnership requires considerable perception on both sides so that not everything has to be verbalised. I remember with MacMillan, right from the beginning, we often had very little to say and the understanding of the work grew as we went along. But as we have begun more complex work, of course a great deal of investigation and discussion is needed in order to achieve a solution to the problems which arise on such productions.

A S: Does the choreographer always take the initiative?

Barry Kay: No. It's possible that various ideas may come from the designer. This happens quite often. MacMillan in particular has a gift of being able to take a given idea, to absorb it, and to integrate it so well into a production that you can't tell from where it has originated.

On the other hand he frequently offers the most excellent design suggestions. By the end of a production there is such a fusion of ideas that you could never tell where they all began.

A S: You have decided, the two of you, to do a ballet and

the ideas start springing out. In the practical sense what happens?

Barry Kay: Right from the beginning?

A S: Right from the beginning.

Barry Kay: Can I say one thing? You have been asked by the choreographer because he knows you are the right choice for a particular production. This is one of the reasons, as I have said before, that there isn't all that much need for verbalising from the beginning. In any case you are likely to be in agreement because of the similar viewpoints which have brought you together in the first place. We usually begin with a general discussion about the production. Then I put very rough ideas together which have probably formulated during our initial talk. Invariably I need to go through a long digestion period. Not necessarily putting ideas down on paper, rather thinking and mulling them over. But I have to do this for quite a long time.

A S: How long? Months or weeks?

Barry Kay: It could be weeks but usually longer. In the case of *Isadora* which we are working on now, it was many months as it is such a complex production. It did require a lot more thinking in order to arrive at a total – so that I didn't see it in parts. This is always the danger in a large work, a full length production with numerous scenes – that you will see it in sections. You mustn't. No matter

how sketchy, it is essential to visualize a total from early on.

Next come quite rough notes. I never make anything too elaborate at the beginning in order not to frighten myself – so just rough sketches that can be torn up – and when I feel that there is an idea emerging, I go back to a discussion with the choreographer. More often than not I find that we are much agreed, that we have been thinking along similar lines.

This was much the case when I designed Kenneth MacMillan's production of *The Sleeping Beauty*, for the Deutsche Oper in Berlin. He was then Director of the Ballet Company and had invited me to Berlin in order to exchange ideas on the way in which the production might be mounted. I had thought of transposing the story from France to Russia, making it closer to the music of Tchaikovsky. Traditionally it has always been set in the French Court of the 17th Century with the awakening taking place in the 18th Century. My proposal was to set it all a century later commencing with the Court of Catherine the Great. In this way the court's awakening would be contemporary to Tchaikovsky's score.

To my surprise, when I arrived in Berlin, I found that

The Sleeping Beauty. Berlin 1967. Act III model

we had been thinking along very similar lines, especially over repatriating the work to Russia.

A S: We'll talk about costume in detail in a moment, but nowadays designers tend to do all the production, both the scenery and the costumes, don't they?

Barry Kay: Yes, on the whole.

A S: But would you be against one person designing the scenery and another the costume?

Barry Kay: Well it depends. If the work is stylised with inventive sets and costumes, then certainly there needs to be a total cohesion between the two elements – this is something requiring a single vision. However, in a production which is more realistic in style, I can imagine that it wouldn't be necessary. For instance, if you had historical costumes which fitted into an equally realistic setting, then I could imagine it possibly being designed by two people. The only thing is that I have never done that myself and I don't think I would ever want to do it that way. To give another example, the production of *Isadora* which I am currently designing, requires costumes of a documentary nature and a contrasting set. To bring the two together successfully, I need a grasp of the whole concept as there is a fine balance to be considered when you are combining such disparate elements.

A S: So how do you begin?

Barry Kay: I usually commence with the sets. I think I've hardly ever begun with the costumes. The sets act as a base from which the rest develops. Usually I find it easier to work with rough bits and pieces – scraps of card or wood, just to see something in the round. This is in order to have some idea of how I might use the space. I have always felt more comfortable working in a sculptural way rather than going direct to the drawing board. I tend to alternate between building things very roughly (to see a shape within the given space) and making drawings which further those ideas. I develop them simultaneously. But in formulating a design, the most important element remains the sculptural or architectural one, as you've probably noticed from my rather constructivist sets.

As I'm dealing with something three-dimensional, I find it confining just working it out on paper. It would all remain too flat when starting to build the actual model.

Of course I'm talking about the proscenium stage. But this applies even more with the theatre-in-the-round where you're obliged to conceive the design in a three-dimensional way. I remember when I began designing for the international opera houses that they were still used to using flat painted scenery for the ballet. Ballet design in the classical tradition continued to be influenced by Diaghilev's use of easel painters. Other developments which had taken place during the twenties were forgotten. When I produced my first design for

Covent Garden – *Images of Love*, it was not easy for them to accept a completely built set. And to begin with, I encountered even more resistance to change from opera houses on the Continent.

It's this structural side to design that has largely motivated my continuing interest in ballet. The limitations of ballet design are unique and I suppose that I've always found these limitations a challenge. You are faced with this dance space that must be kept quite free while at the same time attempting to create a convincing location. The more realistic the environment, the greater the problem. There are various devices which I have worked on and developed over the years, particularly in the use of the space overhead.

These constructions above the dance area serve to describe what might exist upon it without actually having to be put there, except perhaps for a few props. Quite often you find variations on ceilings and other more abstracted structures in my sets.

A S: And it's into this setting that you put the dancers?

The Sleeping Beauty. Berlin 1967. Carabosse Act I *(right)*

The Sleeping Beauty. Berlin 1967. Carabosse Act I design

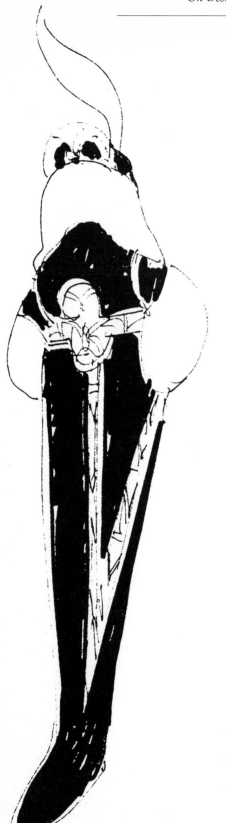

Barry Kay: Yes. Coming back to costume! We've veered a great deal, but it does relate to costume, for besides any other consideration I also do this so as to bring the costumes into as close a relation with the sets as possible, whether the purpose be for unity or contrast.

A S: What are the particular problems of dance costume?

Barry Kay: The biggest one lies in the fact that there are enormous limitations as to what you can do on a dancer's body. That's one of the first problems you face. In the classical ballet there is one of the greatest restrictions. The *tutu*. What do you do with a *tutu*? It's a shape which you can only vary slightly – so basic that there is just a question of what pattern will go on top of it. Early on, I actually learned a great deal from *Haute Couture*. I used to go frequently to fittings at various couturiers in order to study how they constructed costume. Their approach to it was quite architectural, which had greater appeal to me, than what I had seen of ordinary dress-making methods. I felt I could learn more from the couturiers about the disciplines of proportion, line and form, and I've tried very much to bring that into the theatre. They have a special finesse in construction. It's not the detailing that goes into the making so much as the attitude towards the building of a costume. It's something which influenced me greatly. Equally important for me is drawing. Not that I think it is necessarily a pre-requisite for good design, but I think it is a great help in understanding proportions and being able to deal with the body to best advantage. Not only that, a good drawing is a greater incentive to the maker in many respects. It is something I chose to study and to practise from quite early on. In any case, I have always been conscious of the fact that most of the best designs in the past have been produced by those who were also excellent draughtsmen – from the Bibienas to Bakst.

A S: How detailed does the drawing need to be?

Barry Kay: Well I have a sort of shorthand in my drawings so that the design can be understood immediately by the maker. I don't need to make extra working drawings. But that's taken years of working out. A direct approach with a limited amount of detailed explanation.

A S: So then the drawing is agreed upon, the final design is agreed by the choreographer?

Barry Kay: Yes.

A S: And then it goes to the workroom? Do they make patterns first, how do they proceed?

Anastasia. Kschessinka, evening coat, back view, preliminary sketch

Barry Kay: Yes. They usually make up *toiles*, which is also similar to couture. From those *toiles* they begin work on the actual costume. One of the major factors of course is the understanding of what material will do in movement. In that respect it is vital that the designer has a thorough knowledge of material. In order to make a successful ballet costume, it probably comes before anything else, because if you've chosen the wrong material then, no matter how good your cut is, it's not going to work at all as a dance costume.

A S: You therefore detail the material the costume is to be made in, and all the trimmings?

Barry Kay: Yes, all the materials have to be selected and this is a very long process. When all the designs are assembled you begin to select, largely through pattern books or materials which happen to be available in the theatre's stockroom – they usually keep quite a large stock of materials, but you always have to obtain the bulk of it from other sources. While I'm designing I have a very clear idea all the time about the type of fabric I intend using. It's by force of habit – not something I am all that conscious of; it's just there while I'm working on the designs.

A S: Do you find these materials on the market?

Barry Kay: Sometimes they have to be imported.

A S: Do some of your designs require special fabrics?

Barry Kay: Very often. I don't always use material straight. That is to say, sometimes it needs to be combined with other materials, overlays and appliqués to destroy that 'dressmakerish' look that material can often have on the stage unless it is treated in various ways. Sometimes it's with dyeing. The texture is very important on stage, particularily in relation to how it reads at a distance.

A S: What materials are generally used for dance?

Barry Kay: That varies considerably. Of course net is always used for the classical *tutu*. But for other costumes, it all depends on the quality of movement required. There are certain materials such as chiffon, silk and organza which move better than others, but on the whole, in terms of movement there is a rather limited choice. Numerous variations exist within the same range of fabric, but in actual fact the number of different materials available is not great.

Speaking of limitations, there is another which is considerable – the narrow possibilities that exist in constructing a dancer's costume. Not only is it a question of adapting to movement or being familiar with the way in which the body works. To realise any successful costume, a well structured costume, there must be an understanding of the divisions which most enhance the dancer's body – which lines and their placement look best both in cut and ornament. A designer can bring his individual style to solving this problem as well. One of the most common mistakes can arise when a painter or sculptor, not previously experienced in the technicalities of costume making, is commissioned to design a production. There is often a tendency to pin a drawing directly to the body – to project the two-dimensional picture straight onto the figure without fully taking into account that there is also a back and sides. This is one of the reasons that Diaghilev employed Chanel to aid as an adviser on various occasions, as painters were frequently invited to design for his company.

Yet another aspect lies in the relation of the design to the individual who is wearing it. I find that there is often the need to allow for a margin of change, but this is usually in the case of soloists. It's really a matter of knowing how to retain the essentials of a design without imposing something which doesn't suit the dancer. Sometimes this involves problems in movement.

A S: You get to know this movement?

Barry Kay: Yes, or by knowing the choreographer's work. It's not always necessary to see the choreography at first, although more often than not I would say it is essential. It depends. If you take one of the classical productions such as *Sleeping Beauty* or *Swan Lake*, you are dealing with a known quantity, but with an original work there is likely to be a wider range of alternatives when it comes to style of presentation. However, this depends on the choreographer's approach to a new work and whether he has formulated a precise visual concept which he needs interpreting or whether he requires the additional vision of the designer with whom he has chosen to work.

A S: Have you ever found that you've made a complete mistake?

Barry Kay: Once, only once. But it was certainly complete as it involved the entire set of costumes for the ballet *Cain and Abel* which I designed for the Deutsche Oper in Berlin. Unfortunately I hadn't seen the choreography because at the time I was also working in London. I had completed the designs and been over quite briefly for a number of fittings but without having seen rehearsals. I arrived for the dress rehearsal, we sat there and the curtain went up. There were all these costumes glaring at us, entirely wrong for the choreography. Besides the surprise, I remember it was quite mesmerising. Anyway we scrapped them and overnight came up with something completely different. The wardrobe was remarkably helpful. It was somewhat traumatic, but we re-did it. I must say that's the only time it has ever happened.

A S: Was that because you had not been in touch together?

Preliminary drawings for *Anastasia* Act I, Royal Ballet 1971

BARRY KAY: Russian wooden churches: that was the first reference material I began to look at. I was, at that stage, very fascinated by the construction of these churches. There were certain elements in the structure which I wondered whether I could incorporate into the design. I made several drawings. From these came the idea of the wood, the chopped-down birch trees, that come from the sawn off beam ends which cross on the churches. That led me towards finding a way of incorporating wood into the screens. I was trying to bring two disparate elements together. Finally, I found a way in which I could marry the two by pushing the trees through the screens until they became a kind of vortex in the last act. I tried to make the design expressive of the situation in which the Tzar and his family were trapped.

There was something about the shape of the domes of the churches that suggested the curves that I finally used in the screens. Although the final design is quite different when you come to look at it- the domes were actually a starting point. My original interest in the churches came from childhood when we were living in Switzerland. My parents used to visit some members of the Tzar's family who had escaped in the Revolution. I think it was Princess Tatiana who used to make some ravishing small postcards; all highly coloured with these wooden constructions and little golden domes in the snow. That is really what started me off. I used to be fascinated by them as a child.

Barry Kay: It was a mistake because I should have been on the spot during most of the preparation. This is why I usually devote the maximum amount of time to one production without other distractions. On this rare occasion I was obliged to divide my time. Needless to say I don't any more.

A S: Do you find at all that some costumes have to be adapted once they're made, that they have to be changed during performance? The dancer may be happy in dress rehearsal but . . .

Barry Kay: Not really, because I find that I solve most of the problems which arise in the fitting room with the dancer. An experienced dancer is usually quite confident in what you're doing, or have designed. I rarely have difficulties in this direction because I'm always conscious of the dancers' problems and incorporate this into the supervision of the work, so that – unless I find there's

some psychological barrier – it's usually straightforward

One of the most excellent people to design for is Margo Fonteyn as she possesses perfect proportions. I have never met another dancer, either male or female, who has such proportions, so that when you're at a fitting it's patently clear where things have gone wrong. Her body

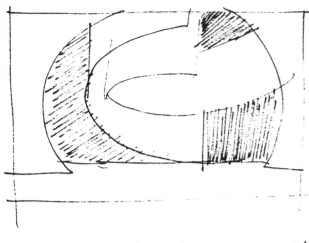

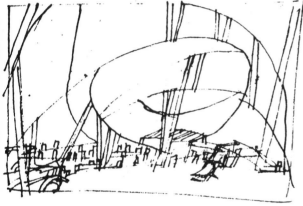

seems to make everything look clumsy if there's the slightest mistake but immaculate when it's right.

A S: Do you approach every ballet in a similar way?

Barry Kay: No, not at all. Each time it's a new solution.

A S: When you're designing a classic are you influenced by previous productions? Are you aware of previous solutions?

Barry Kay: Yes I am. But I'm not influenced. I mean the influence could be to go in quite another direction. With *Sleeping Beauty* for instance, it was an interesting example. Having had a musical background, I have always given special attention to the music. So I took the cue from Tchaikovsky's score and thought there was a curious discrepancy between the French Court in which the production is usually set and the 'Russian-ness' of the music. I listened to the music many times over and felt that somehow there must be a way of getting closer to this 'Russian-ness'. And then I began to look at a lot of material, architectural mostly, and saw a way of bringing it together in a Russian Court setting. Now there was one

thing I knew which MacMillan wanted to do from the beginning. He wished to create a big contrast between the people of the Court and the fairytale figures in order to have two distinct levels in the ballet and not one as is usual. In this way it would lend an unexpected weight to the production. I've always found a certain barbaric quality in the music, which doesn't suggest anything particularly French. This quality seemed a perfect foil for the golden vaulted setting which I now envisaged. It would also heighten the filagree quality of the enamelled fairy costumes. The courtiers' costumes were literally built.

Huge encrusted panniers were weighted with fur in order to accentuate the delicacy of the fairy costumes. At the outset, the director of the theatre was decidedly against the whole concept. He felt convinced that I was designing for a film studio, not a theatre and least of all for a ballet company. One of the major objections was that with such weight and elaboration in both sets and costumes – one would defeat the other, the result being indigestible to the eye. But I knew that the total effect would be a cohesive one in which the overall encrustation becomes a harmonising texture.

Then after all the battles to mount our production were over, on the first night, the director came up to me and generously conceded – 'You know we never thought it possible, but it works. It does work.'

This *Sleeping Beauty* was one of the largest theatre productions to have been seen in Germany since the war.

A S: What about completely new ballets?

Barry Kay: Yes, where you're working in unknown territory.

A S: The choreographer has an idea to do a new ballet. What happens then?

Barry Kay: Can I talk about *Isadora* which I am now designing. For this production we have been working from a scenario by Gillian Freeman. A very complete script and more than any outline I have worked with previously on a ballet.

Although it's unusual, the method is suited to such a narrative work. In some ways it is like a miniature film script, partly because of the numerous sequences. An idea had evolved for the sets which seemed workable and this would accommodate all the scene changes, so we decided that it was the way to continue and I developed the model to a state of completion. Then as MacMillan began to work on his choreography, something appeared to be too static about the concept. There wasn't sufficient flexibility for the fluidity which was now emerging in both choreography and production. After such a long period absorbing the original idea, we were both tentative about admitting the need for a re-think. But while MacMillan worked with the scenario, scenes were merging in a less realistic manner than anticipated, and this greater freedom reflected very much on the way in which I had designed the sets. So with a deep breath, we decided on a total re-design which I started only a couple of weeks ago. So you see such things happen of which an audience is quite unaware.

This kind of reconsideration is far less likely with costume. There's the one example I've cited, but usually

Liz da Costa. *Photo: Moira Walters* *(right)*

Isadora. Preliminary sketch for Isadora Act II 1927. Royal Ballet 1971

planning takes place over a long period and the costumes tend to come later not only because of the working method but the dancers' availability for fitting has also to be considered. For most ballets the making of the costumes is condensed into a shorter period than the rest of the production and often commences towards the latter part of its preparation. On almost every ballet production I have worked, the last four weeks is the crucial period for the costumes.

A S: Do you find that you tend to work with the same costume makers?

Barry Kay: Obviously you develop certain favourites. That happens. Nowadays, not necessarily a great deal of work is done within the opera house itself. As you know, I work mostly for opera houses and in a certain number of these theatres like those in Vienna, Paris or Berlin, they do the greatest part in their workshops, but at Covent Garden it's not always possible. Quite often there are many outworkers, so you find some people who are better at interpreting your work than others and naturally I try to work with them if possible. The theatre fortunately understands that and makes it possible for those costumiers to be employed.

A S: Presumably you are given a budget to work to?

Barry Kay: Yes, but on certain productions this has not always been so clearly defined. Normally the managements have a reasonably clear idea of the average cost of a production, depending on its size and this is weighed up against the knowledge they have about a designer's previous work. Each department must also assess its own estimate of costs. The wardrobe supervisor will do this basically from the cast list. It is reasonably simple to gauge the average cost of a ballet costume which must include wigs, shoes and accessories. But with the sets it is a more complicated process because the individual parts are always different and the costing depends not only on the materials required for their making but also on their size. If special mechanical devices are part of the scheme, then these are also included in the total budget.

Should the designs appear to be going in excess of the budget, then the management will ask what you can do to help. This means looking at the drawings and models and somehow you usually find ways around it. With experience you discover that it is not always necessary to stick to the letter. In the beginning I used to become easily disheartened over changes, but later you find that there is always an alternative to most problems. As Picasso said, 'When you don't have blue use red' or vice versa. It *is* like that, you know. Adapt to the means. The most important thing is the idea, that's what matters. Of course it's fine if you have all the freedom of an unlimited budget. But above all it's still the quality of ideas which is the essence.

24 October 1980. London

Liz da Costa completed a degree course at Central School of Art and Design. She was awarded an Arts Council Designer's Bursary and worked with the Royal Exchange Theatre in Manchester designing *Last Resort* for Peter Flannery. Returning to London she designed *The Changeling* at Riverside Studios, and *Nice* for Mustapha Matura. Other theatre work includes Unicorn Theatre, Soho Poly, New End, Nottingham Playhouse, The Roundhouse, Lyric Studio, and the English Theatre in Vienna. Dance theatres include Extemporary, Contemporary, Emma, Rambert, Junction and Mantis.

She has taught Theatre Design at Hounslow Borough College and was invited to Central School and RADA as guest designer. She has contributed work to the Gold Medal Prague Quadrienale exhibition currently on tour, and is in the process of setting up a design and production team.

Liz da Costa: I went to Central School of Art and Design where I did a Foundation Course followed by three years training in Theatre Design.

A S: What made you choose Theatre Design?

Liz da Costa: Working three-dimensionally was always of interest. That was the initial reason for going to art school. It was the first time I had the opportunity to experiment; every day was given to actually trying things

out, which was not possible previously due to the fact that art had always been considered, at least in my experience, a 'Friday Afternoon' subject of little importance at school. Theatre design seemed to combine all the various elements I wanted.

A S: Why did you particularly want to work in the theatre?

Liz da Costa: I suppose it's because I had a basic interest in plays, and all that area entails. Producing something and seeing it realized. I wanted to make a constructive contribution to the development of a play.

A S: You didn't want to be a lonely artist?

Liz da Costa: No. I didn't fancy a garret life, but thinking about it, it has become a lonely life with unsocial hours,

but that's another story. In the process of design you are in fact designing on your own before taking it to the theatre.

A S: And after the Central School what happened?

Liz da Costa: I was awarded an Arts Council Designer's Bursary and I spent a year with The Royal Exchange in Manchester. When I left I designed *The Changeling* for Peter Gill at Riverside Studios.

Then I met Micha Bergese, the choreographer, though at that time he was still dancing with Contemporary Dance. Dance was something I had not thought of particularly. It seemed important to keep as many options open as possible, the idea being that the experience gained in one area would feed back into the other. I was quite nervous as to how exactly to approach the first piece. It was a theatre approach and not a dance approach.

A S: Because you didn't know about dance?

Liz da Costa: I had no idea. I had only done work that

Preliminary design for *Solo Ride* (*below and right*)

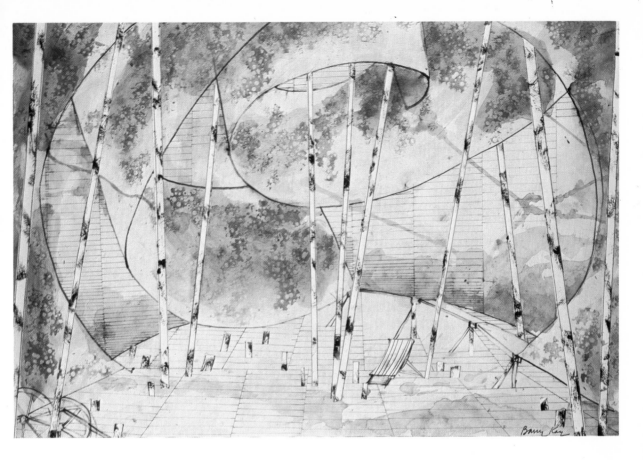

Anastasia. Act I finished design. Royal Ballet 1971

Anastasia. Act I model. Royal Ballet 1971

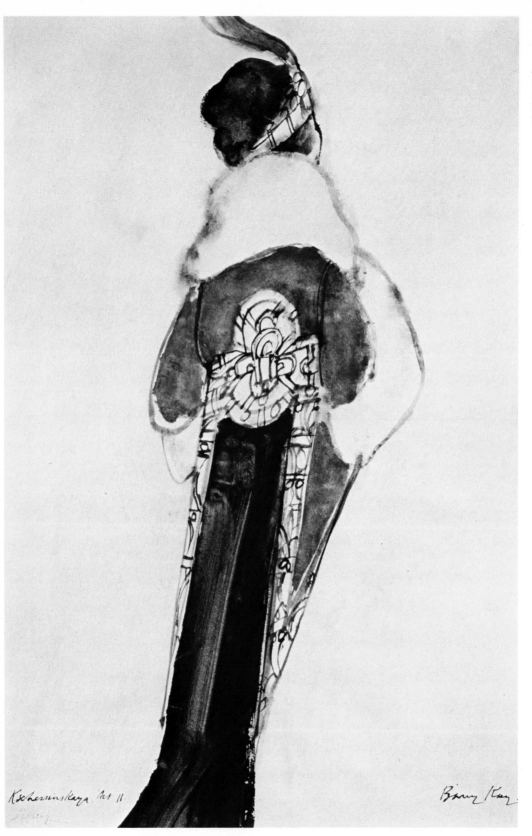

Anastasia.
Kschessinska,
evening coat,
back view. Royal
Ballet 1971

Kschessinskaya Act II.

Barry Kay

Anastasia.
Kschessinska,
evening dress
and coat,
front view.
Royal Ballet 1971

Isadora. Costume design for Isadora Act II 1927. Royal Ballet 1981

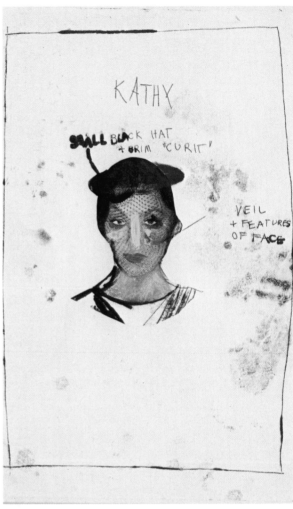

Hat and make-up design for *Scene Shift*

included dance, never dance exclusively. It had had a reference point but working for Contemporary Dance seemed a jump in the deep end.

A S: What was the first ballet you designed?

Liz da Costa: It was called *Solo Ride*.

A S: How did you start? By talking to the choreographer?

Liz da Costa: Yes, but talking to a choreographer as I would talk to a director. I think that there's nothing special in the fact that it's dance or theatre. It's all the same process. The difference was that we didn't start with a script, we evolved one. I began to sit in on all the rehearsals to see what was suggested by the movement.

A S: What was his idea for the ballet?

Liz da Costa: Well, quite honestly it was very vague at the beginning. That was the problem. You're suddenly confronted with no script, no nothing, and a lot of movement happening from which you can only get certain images or ideas. But as far as having an initial idea, that didn't exist. I had to try to pin him down to something in particular.

A S: After quite a long time?

Liz da Costa: Quite a long time. Because there was only one man and four women, the dance seemed to suggest his relationship to them. I suppose anything you start with will inevitably change, trying different movements until the combination is right.

A S: At what stage did you start thinking about appropriate designs?

Liz da Costa: I tried to produce something for him to react against. I did a series of drawings and we laid them out on the studio floor, and went through them.

A S: How did he react?

Liz da Costa: He rejected various shapes and ideas. The dancers' movements had suggested certain things from the twenties, and I tried to find a shape that would retain

that idea. There was also the idea that the male figure was a very lonely one, and the idea that he danced with his alter ego, a dummy, at the end was symbolic of his total rejection of everyone else. It developed like that. We also tried to think of a way of having the musicians on stage. It seemed that the music needed to be seen, the orchestra pit always seems to remove the musicians from what is really going on. To have the music and dancer playing alongside each other seemed a better way of connecting the piece as a whole. The set was basically a large brick wall which ran along the back, with an area for the musician to sit in. Contemporary Dance rarely consider having a set. I think it took them somewhat by surprise when I arrived clutching my model.

A S: Was the musician costumed as well?

Liz da Costa: Yes. He was bowler hatted and suited. He was a city gent. He was just sitting in his brick wall. The other thing that interested me about dance was how dancers got on to the stage. It seemed that something should be done about their entrance. Not just to break a tradition or a convention or anything, but nobody was actually using the fact that you were dealing with the most agile bodies that could do the most incredible things. Although maybe I shouldn't say it, from what I saw of contemporary dance I felt that it was in a way almost like a feat of gymnastics, just a series of stunning movements. The costumes were really only showing the shape of the dancer, which obviously they should do, but there it had got to the point where there was nothing else they contributed. It was just 'Oh they're in blue today' and 'the next dancer is in a yellow catsuit' and that's it. So my whole idea was to try and break out of as many conventions and traps as I could. There was a fair bit of criticism about what I did because I put them in baggy trousers and oversuits and things like that. My way to get Tom, the male figure, onto the stage was by bicycle which he rode with his dummy behind. We introduced the dancers gradually, building up a stage picture before the dance itself began.

A S: So what happened after you displayed your first drawings round the studio? Were some rejected and some accepted?

Liz da Costa: Yes. I would say that 90% were rejected, which was good, because having decided what it was we didn't want we selected something more positive to work towards. Anyway, we didn't need all those costumes. We finalised a shape and idea. After more drawings the definitive shape emerged. By watching more rehearsals, the movements suggested certain elements to incorporate in the colouring and the style of the costumes. It suddenly seemed very cartoon like. I tried to transfer

Some Dance, Some Duet. Photo: Anthony Crickmay

ideas suggested by the movement by drawing directly on to the costume. For instance, a couple of dancers used their hands very much more than anyone else so I tried to emphasize that idea by drawing their hands onto their costumes. It was a very stylized piece in its movement, and the two dimensional graphic approach to the costumes added to that. It was also an attempt to reproduce a drawing onto a costume.

A S: How successful was it?

Liz da Costa: I think it was successful considering it was my first dance piece. And I think that right, wrong or indifferent we had achieved what we set out to do. Perhaps it was also of interest to people who came to expect something quite specific from Contemporary Dance. The set provided the audience with another aspect, so I think it served a purpose on that level as well. As always, it's hard not to fall back into the conventional. Suddenly you became a dance person and it's hard, when you have continual criticism about a baggy costume or something, to produce work that's still interesting or different enough. I think it's a trap you can fall into and we nearly fell into it with that fringed piece, *Some Dance, Some Duet*. The problem is that choreographers tend to do a piece before I design it, or before we've talked. Sometimes it's finished before I even come along.

A S: Would you like to come along earlier?

Liz da Costa: I'd like to talk about the piece as early as possible, no matter how vaguely. At least then the movements are relating to the idea. When confronted with a finished piece that seems to have no basic concept, or one that is not coming through in the dance, its hard to produce an immediate solution.

A S: That's quite exciting though?

Liz da Costa: Yes. Well it's panic time really, because you realise that whatever the costume is, it is also what people are looking at, in spite of the movement. To a certain extent it's what the dancers are moving in or what people are looking at that makes the whole thing work or not, I think. You can't say 'Oh well, we'll do it with lights' because it just doesn't work. There has to be something to light. So when I was confronted with all that movement, it was difficult to find an image for the piece. There was no basis for it. So, realising that you were abstracting something before you'd even started, you were working from nothing, I just thought of something that would add as much movement as possible and I decided to use fringes. It started off with the idea of an art deco sculpture and the idea that the girls' dresses would have layers and layers of fringe that would actually 'take off' – rather like the ideas of Oskar Schlemmer. These fringes would revolve round a shape, adding another dimension to the movement. The good thing about theatre is that if somebody has to wear a long dress then they rehearse, or you try to make them rehearse, in a long dress. The actor then incorporates the costume into his movements, but in this case costume and dancer didn't come together until the last minute. So when I produced these rather unusual costumes everybody panicked. There were a couple of dresses, very heavily fringed dresses, which I realised as soon as I saw them that there was no way the girls were going to cope with. They were already worried about the dance, amongst other things, and there wasn't time to evolve the costume within the framework of the dance. It was too isolated. The costumes had to be simplified. And the fringes for the men's costumes were sewn into a catsuit – which is the first catsuit, I confess, I've used. For me it was a bit disappointing because I quite liked the idea of what I had set out to do, which was to extend the movement. But the costumes became very much more minimal and in cutting them back they lost something.

A S: On the practical side, do you do a lot of drawing?

Liz da Costa: Less and less, as I do more and more things, which is a shame because the sort of little Utopia in which one spent one's training, where one had time to sit down and spend six weeks on producing something that one felt with a certain amount of conviction was the right thing simply does not exist. When, in practice, you literally have a day or two in which to produce something you rely on instinct. It's good and bad. You're continually aware of new possibilities. At the same time, I think it's sad because what you're actually showing the audience isn't as well thought out as you'd like it to be. I have to have the opportunity of developing certain ideas into the next piece. I was doing that with *Scene Shift*, which was the piece after *Solo Ride*, because the shapes that are used there, the materials and the ideas of how to use theatre in dance was really an extension of the first work. Ever since then it's been very much more minimal – working with a lot more smaller companies.

A S: What other companies have you worked with?

Liz da Costa: With Emma – East Midlands Arts, Junction, Contemporary, X6, Rambert and Extemporary, 'Mantis', Jumpers.

A S: Mostly with ballet now?

Liz da Costa: No, not really mostly with ballet. Ballet is one side of my work. The rest is still theatre. The two things are beginning to cross. I certainly don't want to be classified as a dance designer, any more than I want to be classified as a theatre designer. I'd like to try and find a medium, like opera, where you could involve all the things.

A S: Have you done any opera?

Liz da Costa: No, but I think that or a film would be a very interesting next step.

A S: So, you make a lot of drawings. Presumably you discuss the drawings with the choreographer and come

to an agreement about them. Then do you make working drawings, do you re-draw, do you make more detailed drawings?

Liz da Costa: Eventually I make a final drawing and we try to find suitable materials. A visit to the wardrobe is next on the list in the case of a large production – otherwise you end up going back to your flat and cutting the costumes out. Apart from conveying ideas to the director it is important to give the people who make the costumes as much information as possible. So that, too is one of the reasons why I like to do a finished drawing. The people who make the costumes like it on their wall and it's something they can look at. They really are the only people you ever draw for because no one else ever sees it. There is no other function for a drawing other than to give instructions about how it should be made. In talking, other ideas may occur. Maybe I thought of a material they've not used before and they think there's no way to use it. Obviously, they're very much more technical than I am, but at the same time, if they do what some carpenters and wardrobe people do – drawing their breath between their teeth and saying – 'I couldn't do that' – you have to be determined. There has to be give and take. Then we talk about it and try to find the solution. With certain costumes it's necessary to make a calico shape first to see if the idea is even feasible. When you translate a two-dimensional drawing into a three-dimensional costume then unforeseen problems tend to arise.

A S: But you don't worry about the cut?

Liz da Costa: Oh yes, I worry about the cut; not so much in the drawing stage, but after that. It's important that the shape you end with interprets the idea as nearly as possible. You have to be adamant in the wardrobe as to exactly what you are aiming towards otherwise your original ideas may be distorted. Then, having made up a calico shape, you start with the fittings and that can change things radically. For example, in the case of the fringes, they looked originally like something out of the 'Addams family' – smothered in fringe. I gave them haircuts and I enjoyed doing that. I actually formed the shapes round the bodies and just kept snipping until they could move freely.

A S: How do the dancers approach their costumes?

Liz da Costa: They always dread it. They are the worst people in the world to fit because they are always moving or creaking.

A S: But they should have good bodies.

Liz da Costa: They have good bodies, but they usually arrive in bad condition. It's usually the end of the day when they're fairly exhausted. It was a nightmare getting

Celia Hulton and Tom Jobe in *Solo Ride*. Photo: Anthony Crickmay

them into those fringed things because we had about twelve people in the room all trying on the costumes at the same time. It wasn't easy. But dancers also have very little patience anyway. Whereas an actor will be quite happy to stand in front of a mirror and let you fiddle around for hours, a dancer is very fidgety. You've got about fifteen minutes for a fitting and you'll be hard-pushed to get the dancers back again or try something different, the schedule is horrendously pressurized, and for those fifteen minutes so are you!

A S: And what if a dancer hates the costume?

Liz da Costa: Well maybe I've been very lucky, I've never had that experience. They are usually sobbing about their solos, and how they don't like the dances. You just say 'Don't worry, you look wonderful' and carry on. No, I've never had that problem. I think I've always confused them. I've always managed to reassure them. 'What's this about?' they say. I try and spout on, buy them a coca-cola and tell them. Try not to use them as puppets. Try to involve them in what's going on and show them the drawings too, so that the costume is not a shock. I think that's quite a nice idea.

A S: Do you think certain materials are more suited to dance than others?

Liz da Costa: I think obviously the most suitable material for dance, no matter how you fight it, is lycra. Because it is so stretchy and malleable. And there are other materials like silks which flow well. I also try to find material which no one has ever used though not solely for reasons of novelty, but because they may work. The fact that one thinks of silk or lycra immediately puts one back into thinking conventionally, because there are limited ways of using those two materials. It's an advantage if one can find a new material as it gives another approach.

A S: Do you have a very strict budget to work to?

Liz da Costa: Yes. The major problem is the budget. If one has time it's possible to do things with a small budget. Without time there is no way. But somehow we've always managed. Shortage of time is a much worse problem than a tight budget. I think the smaller the budget the more inventive you can become. A big budget and you think 'Oh I'll have another hundred metres of silk', rather than think of anything else. But I have never had that problem!

A S: Have you never thought or dreamed about doing *Sleeping Beauty*?

Liz da Costa: No, I can't say I have. It would be quite a challenge. I don't think it would come out quite as people intended. Maybe that's no bad thing.

A S: So you think there are preconceived notions about the great classics?

Liz da Costa: I think it's inevitable because the audience that is going to see a great classic expects to see certain things. That's why they are going to see that sort of work. I think that both the production and the audience have preconceived ideas.

A S: But would you ignore that?

Liz da Costa: I don't think one could ignore it completely. Perhaps one could infiltrate to a certain extent. I don't think there would be any point in doing another *Sleeping Beauty* unless one could add something new to it. Otherwise you are just repeating what's gone before.

A S: Have you ever designed a ballet where you've suddenly realised that everything is wrong?

Liz da Costa: Not that everything is wrong, but that a certain percentage is wrong, yes! Or at least that you've lost track of exactly what the hell is going on. It was like that with *Scene Shift*. We came out of it by the skin of our teeth, but really lack of time meant that we were unable to sift through the new ideas that had occurred during production. We started with the idea that it was going to be a piece about making a film. It was to use the whole company, which was quite a marathon in itself.

A S: How big was the company?

Liz da Costa: 14 or 15. It wasn't quite *Sleeping Beauty*! But it was, on our scale and our budget, a large undertaking. Everybody was to be an integral part of a movie. People in or out of costume, coming and going as they would in a film studio. It became something very different from what everybody had thought of at first. That was a piece one would have liked to have gone on with or scrubbed out completely. It would have been better not to be left as it was. People had their own ideas as to what they enjoyed, but didn't know for what reason.

A S: You would prefer to know more about the intentions of the choreographer?

Liz da Costa: Yes, or at least I'd prefer to have the time in order to suggest things to the choreographer. I definitely dislike the fact that, at times, one goes into a studio after the piece is finished. Then you end up staring at your bookshelves for inspiration in order to find a way of illustrating what it is all about.

A S: The choreographer just thinks of movement?

Liz da Costa: To a certain extent, yes. Contemporary dance tends more towards the abstract and the designer's function is to put that into context.

A S: How much are you affected by the music?

Liz da Costa: A great deal. I think you have to be affected by the music. All things have to become one. So far the choice of music has been fairly quirky, and modern. You can't completely go against it so it becomes a question of relating the music to the final costume, unless there is a strong reason to do otherwise.

A S: And do you listen to the music a lot?

Liz da Costa: No, not a great deal. When I'm at home I listen to it as much as possible, but there's usually only one tape of it and as the dancers are using it there is not much opportunity. Perhaps with *Sleeping Beauty* you could have it thumping through your headphones as you went to sleep.

A S: So your ideas come from watching the rehearsal?

Liz da Costa: There are always some unrealised ideas at the back of your mind you'd like to try out and dance is one of the few areas where there is an opportunity to experiment. It seems that you keep a store of ideas in mind, and, both in theatre and dance, you will eventually get a chance to use them somewhere.

A S: This store is in your mind, or do you cut magazines, or newspapers, collect images?

Liz da Costa: I think there's a fair collection of images in my mind. My flat (my tip, my Wuthering Depths) is a fair store too – I collect books, mainly photographic books because I think they're the best reference. Yes, anything that comes to mind. Also there are so many other things I like doing that they all feed back eventually.

A S: What sort of things?

Liz da Costa: Well, at the moment I'm interested in kinetic jewellery, so my idea now is perhaps I'll be able to make an illuminated dance costume and do the whole dance in darkness and just silhouette the figure. Maybe it will happen one day, perhaps it's not a good idea, but it is interesting to consider the possibilities.

A S: Are you inquisitive about techniques?

Liz da Costa: There are many new technical innovations such as lasers, fibre optics, etc which might have interesting potential for dance application.

Anita Griffin, Charlotte Kirkpatrick and Tom Jobe in *Solo Ride*. Photo: Anthony Crickmay

Scene Shift. Photo: Anthony Crickmay

A S: Who gives you the chances?

Liz da Costa: There aren't a lot of opportunities open for using them. Every production creates a certain optimism as to what you could do, that the chance will occur. Dance broke away into being something very experimental and new and exciting but it now seems to have become very stale. Whilst you appreciate why people produce the works they do, it's now time to make a conscious effort again to explore new possibilities of dance. There's nothing around of any real novelty. Yes, they're nice pieces to see but they are actually not saying any more than last year's pieces. There doesn't seem to be a break coming anywhere.

A S: Where does the break come?

Liz da Costa: It comes with somebody taking a risk. It needs a bit of courage and somebody to say 'There you are. Here's a budget. Now . . .' and commissioning you.

A S: Do you think anything is possible in ballet costume?

Liz da Costa: Well, I don't know if anything is possible – I suppose you need to try it before saying anything is impossible. But perhaps if one considers that, apart from the movement, there is the extra dimension of expression, emotion, and the sculptural qualities of figures in space to be considered, more experimental costumes would be possible.

A S: What are the chances for a young designer these days in the theatre?

Liz da Costa: Slim, I would say. Partly because the future at the moment in the theatre is so uncertain. There isn't the money for productions. Apart from anything else, most companies are on the verge of financial collapse and naturally this causes a dearth of opportunity.

A S: How do you get the first job?

Liz da Costa: That is a basic problem. I think it's sad that you sometimes have to wait so long before somebody will take a risk and give you a job.

A S: You think they're unwilling to take the risk?

Liz da Costa: In the commercial theatre I think so, because everybody needs a name to reduce the risk and as a selling point. It's a kind of Catch 22 – they will not employ people without experience and unless they employ you, you can't get experience. But as long as dance continues to exert its fascination people will always be prepared to overcome the problems. The theatre has proved its resilience over the centuries and in spite of all the signs to the contrary it seems to be alive and well and here to stay.

17 November 1980. London